Why School Leaders Need Vision

Why School Leaders Need Vision

Managing Scarcity, Mandates, and Conflicting Goals for Educational Quality

By Bruce S. Cooper, Carlos R. McCray, and Stephen V. Coffin

ROWMAN & LITTLEFIELD
Lanham • Boulder • New York • London

Published by Rowman & Littlefield
A wholly owned subsidiary of The Rowman & Littlefield Publishing Group, Inc.
4501 Forbes Boulevard, Suite 200, Lanham, Maryland 20706
www.rowman.com

Unit A, Whitacre Mews, 26–34 Stannary Street, London SE11 4AB

Copyright © 2017 by Bruce S. Cooper, Carlos R. McCray, and Stephen V. Coffin

All rights reserved. No part of this book may be reproduced in any form or by any electronic or mechanical means, including information storage and retrieval systems, without written permission from the publisher, except by a reviewer who may quote passages in a review.

British Library Cataloguing-in-Publication Information Available

Library of Congress Cataloging-in-Publication Data

Names: Cooper, Bruce S., editor. | McCray, Carlos R., editor. | Coffin, Stephen, 1954– editor.
Title: Why school leaders need vision : managing scarcity, mandates, and conflicting goals for educational quality / [edited by] Bruce S. Cooper, Carlos R. McCray, and Stephen Coffin.
Description: Lanham : Rowman & Littlefield, a wholly owned subsidiary of The Rowman & Littlefield Publishing Group, Inc., [2017] | Includes bibliographical references and index.
Identifiers: LCCN 2017027837 (print) | LCCN 2017037039 (ebook) | ISBN 9781475833447 (Electronic) | ISBN 9781475833423 (cloth : alk. paper) | ISBN 9781475833430 (pbk. : alk. paper)
Subjects: LCSH: Educational leadership—United States. | School management and organization—United States.
Classification: LCC LB2805 (ebook) | LCC LB2805 .W483 2017 (print) | DDC 371.2—dc23
LC record available at https://lccn.loc.gov/2017027837

Printed in the United States of America

Contents

Foreword   vii
Virginia Roach

1   Visionary Leadership Adds Value   1
    Bruce S. Cooper and Carlos R. McCray

2   Building a Collaborative Visionary Community   5
    Karen Andronico

3   Visionary School Finance Leadership in a "Capped" Fiscal Environment   21
    Stephen V. Coffin

4   Visionary School Leaders for the Twenty-First Century in Special Education   31
    Su-Je Cho, Kwang-Sun Cho Blair, and Holly Rittenhouse-Cea

5   Improving Student Outcomes through Reflective Practice and Mindfulness in Educational Leadership   51
    Lisa Bass

6   Visionary Leadership for Diversity in K–12 Schools: Looking Back to Move Forward   65
    Floyd D. Beachum and Carlos R. McCray

7   Visionary Curriculum: A Journey, Not a Destination   79
    Selma K. Bartholomew and Ingrid Lafalaise

8	Putting Vision into Practice: Exploring Five Timeless Principles for Student Achievement *Jonathan W. Shute*	97
9	The Future with Visionary Leadership in Education—Now! *Carlos R. McCray & Bruce S. Cooper*	113
Index		115
About the Editors		123
About the Contributors		125

Foreword

Visionary leaders in education are those educators who are able to imagine and seek a different future for their schools, teachers, and students. Whether the school is working: (1) to keep students engaged, (2) to ensure learning objectives are met, and/or (3) to develop new community partnerships, visionary leaders paint a picture of a new reality—and work collaboratively with students, faculty, and families to make this vision a reality.

The literature is replete with characteristics of visionary leaders as they are described as collaborative, persistent, passionate, and dynamic (Collins, 2001; DuFour & Marzano, 2009; Reeves, 2006; Simon, 2015; Westley & Mintzberg, 1989).

Visionary leaders are also boundary scanners as being interested in the world external to the school as affecting the internal life of the school (Simon, 2015; Westley & Mintzberg, 1989). And their role is more than just to buffer the school from external forces, or to translate external policies into the school environment (Aldrich & Herker, 1977; Honig, 2006; Tushman, 1977). Rather, visionary leaders incorporate the sociological and political dynamic of the larger world into how the needs of the school community can best be addressed—and importantly, how resources can be maximized to support children and families.

One important factor that visionary leaders must attend to is the sociological reality of how those with whom they work approach the world. Why is this so important? Because schools are full of leaders, students, teachers, and parents from different generations. The majority of school leaders (from Generation X) view and experience the world through primarily different assumptions than most teachers and parents (as Millennials or Generation Y) and students (as Generation Z). The very way in which these three sociologically defined generations experience, view, and make sense of the world around them differs in terms of core understandings and beliefs (Pew Research Center, 2014; Strauss & Howe, 1992). These core understandings and beliefs shape vision, strategy, motivation, and how goals are defined. Without understanding these differences, school leaders will find it increasingly difficult to be effective, let alone visionary.

Most school principals belong to Generation X (National Center for Education Statistics 2015). Born between 1960 and 1980 (being in their late thirties to fifties), they are characterized as highly educated, active, balanced, happy, and family-oriented. Their worldview is based on change; the need to combat corruption; and the drive to embrace human dignity, social diversity, tolerance, and individual freedom (Miller, 2013).

These worldviews are expressed in how they act: they seek long-term institutional change through the creation of new structures. Their work in education is characterized by how to implement equity, as seen in their policies that moved from "mainstreaming" students with disabilities into inclusive classrooms. Similarly, this generation has moved away from busing to utilizing magnet schools as a means racially and economically to integrate the schools (Aldridge & Goldman, 2002). Additionally, reflecting their orientation to change, they embraced the charter movement.

In contrast, the majority of school teachers and parents are Millennials (National Center for Education Statistics, 2015). Generation Y/Millennials were born between 1980 and 1995 (twenty-two years old to late thirties). They prefer group consensus to personal risk and tend to be nonconfrontational. They have focused on "No bullying" laws in education policy. Millennials are strongly connected to family and friends. They delayed the five major markers of adulthood: completing school, leaving home, becoming financially independent, marrying, and having children (Pew Research Center 2014).

They believe in giving, and they feel connected to the world in a way that earlier generations did not. Raised in a time of wealth accumulation, Millennials have high career aspirations and are confident and upbeat about their opportunities; however, they often report a bleak job outlook (Furlong & Cartmel, 2007; Pew Research Center, 2010).

Known as the first "digital natives," this generation started with desktop computers, then moved to laptops, and now widely uses mobile devices (Pew Research Center, 2014). Fully 92 percent are engaged in multitasking related to technology and social media, 74 percent get their news from TV and the Internet, and 88 percent of the youngest Millennials get their news from Facebook (Junco & Mastrodicasa, 2007).

Visionary leaders of Generation X must understand and take the worldview of their millennial teachers and students' parents into careful consideration. For this generation, work-life balance is a priority. Millennial teachers respond favorably to short-term intervals of praise, opportunities to work collaboratively in teams, flexible work schedules, coaching and mentoring, and a role in decision-making in the school. In terms of job permanence, Millennials are characterized as flexible, taking career risks and more frequently changing jobs (Furlong & Cartmel, 2007).

Importantly, while Generation X's approach to work is to work smarter through innovation and acquiring additional skills, Millennials are more likely to switch jobs to match the skills they have. Millennials are very willing to work in charter schools, virtual schools, and online as they do not view any single job as a lifetime commitment.

Raised with diversity, they assume the presence of diverse learners in the classroom. Moreover, Millennial teachers and parents are interested in fast-paced results. The Generation X visionary leader must understand and utilize the strengths of these teachers and parents, appreciating the differences between the Millennial and Generation X worldviews.

Ultimately, visionary leaders have to understand their students in order to set a course for the school. It is the students, after all, who are the future. Generationally, the students in schools today predominately belong to Generation Z. Colloquially called the "Zeds," they were born between the mid-1990s and the present. Defined by the Internet and social media, they are the first generation of *Internet natives*. While Millennials started using computers for games, word processing, and rudimentary e-mail, Zeds have been fully immersed in social media from an early age.

Many were exposed to the Internet and social media as toddlers, and they see no difference between the physical and digital world. These children, socialized through the Internet, conduct most of their social life digitally (O'Leary, 2014). While this generation has experienced school "lockdowns," watched their parents get laid off in the 2008 recession, and witnessed the 9/11 attacks on the United States as young children, the digital bond created with the Internet may help them cope with these larger societal stressors (Turner, 2015). Perhaps because of these experiences, Zeds are more risk-averse, more likely to use seatbelts, and less likely to use alcohol (Williams, 2015).

Particularly challenging for the Generation X principal is understanding how to prepare the Zed for the future. Sixty-five percent of Zeds will work in jobs that have yet to be created. Digital technology will be an aspect of every career path for this generation (Henderson, 2013). Like Millennials, this generation is characterized by their versatility, high self-esteem, multitasking abilities, and expectation of flexibility in their environment. In short, the students in schools today have more in common with their millennial teachers and parents than either group has in common with the Generation X principal.

Leaders are not typically expected to gather sociological and political information related to the key stakeholders of the school—students, parents, and teachers. Yet, understanding how to collect and use this information—to create a vision with teachers, parents, and students who do not share the leader's worldview—distinguishes a good leader from a true visionary leader. Visionary leaders must attend to the everyday functioning of the school, respond to external policies and political pressures, recognize the weaknesses in the school and, at the same time, understand the inner- and intergenerational perspectives and strengths of the key stakeholders.

Armed with this information, the visionary leader can imagine and act on a different future for the school and its students. Combining the visionary leader's plan with the collaboration and assistance of teachers, parents, and students helps to make that vision a reality.

Virginia Roach

REFERENCES

Aldrich, H. E., & Herker, D. (1977). Boundary spanning roles and organizational structure. *The Academy of Management Review, 2*(2), 217–230.

Aldridge, J., & Goldman, R. (2002). *Current issues and trends in education*. Boston, MA: Allyn and Bacon.

Collins, J. (2001). *Good to great: Why some companies make the leap . . . and others don't*. New York: HarperCollins Publishers, Inc.

DuFour, R., & Marzano, R. (2009). High leverage strategies for principal leadership. *Educational Leadership, 66*(5), 62–68.

Furlong, A., & Cartmel, F. (2007). *Young people and social change*. (2nd ed.). Berkshire, England: Open University Press/McGraw Hill.

Henderson, J. M. (2013). Move over, Millennials: Why 20-somethings should fear teens. *Forbes*. Retrieved March 15, 2015, from https://www.forbes.com/sites/jmaureenhenderson/2013/07/31/move-over-millennials-why-twentysomethings-should-fear-teens/#79cf3c061d89

Honig, M. (2006). Street-level bureaucrats revisited: Frontline district central office Administrators as boundary spanners in education policy implementation. *Educational Evaluation and Policy Analysis, 28* (4), 357–383.

Junco, R., & Mastrodicasa, J. (2007). *Connecting to the net.generation: What higher education professionals need to know about today's students*. Washington, DC: National Association of Student Personnel Administrators.

Miller, J. D. (2013). Lifelong learning: Generation X illustrates the new reality. *The Generation X Report: Quarterly Research Report from the Longitudinal Study of American Youth*. Ann Arbor, MI: University of Michigan. Retrieved March 15, 2017, from http://www.lsay.org/GenX_Vol2Iss3.pdf

National Center for Education Statistics (2015). Digest of Education Statistics. Table 212.08 Number and percentage distribution of principals in public and private elementary and secondary schools, by selected characteristics: Selected years,

1993–94 through 2011–12. Retrieved March 15, 2017, from https://nces.ed.gov/programs/digest/d15/tables/dt15_212.08.asp?current=yes

O'Leary, H. (2014). Recruiting Gen Z: No more business as usual. Web report. September 23, 2014. Boston, MA: Eduventures. Retrieved March 15, 2017, from http://www.eduventures.com/2014/09/recruiting-gen-z/

Pew Research Center (2010). *Millennials: Confident. Connected. Open to change.* Philadelphia, PA: The Pew Charitable Trusts.

Pew Research Center (2014). Millennials in adulthood: Detached from institutions, networked with friends. Retrieved March 15, 2017, from http://www.pewsocialtrends.org/files/2014/03/2014-03-07_generations-report-version-for-web.pdf

Reeves, D. (2006). *The learning leader.* Alexandria, VA: Association for Curriculum and Supervision.

Simon, F. (2015). Looking up and out to lead: 20/20 vision for effective leadership. *Young Children, 70*(2), 18–24.

Strauss, W., & Howe, N. (1992). *Generations: The history of America's future, 1584 to 2069.* New York: HarperCollins Publishers, Inc.

Turner, A. (2015). Generation Z: Technology and social interest. *Journal of Individual Psychology, 71*(2), 103–113.

Tushman, M. L. (1977). Special boundary roles in the innovation process. *Administrative Science Quarterly, 22*(4), 587–605.

Westley, F., & Mintzberg, H. (1989, June). *Strategic Management Journal, 10,* 17–32.

Williams, A. (2015, September). Move over, Millennials, Here comes Generation Z, *New York Times.* Retrieved March 15, 2017, from https://www.nytimes.com/2015/09/20/fashion/move-over-millennials-here-comes-generation-z.html?r=0

Chapter 1

Visionary Leadership Adds Value

Bruce S. Cooper and Carlos R. McCray

The concept of "visionary" leadership is defined and applied in this book as "supervision in schools" requires a level of *super vision* that can be best developed through quality leadership, mentoring—and mutual ideas and support—for adding more value to the school and its staff and students.

This book shows just how vision is important and useful in all schools and districts—in fact, also, to all communities and families. Former U.S. secretary of education, Arne Duncan, when addressing United Nations in 2010, made it clear that:

> Education is still the key to eliminating gender inequities, to reducing poverty, to creating a sustainable planet, and to fostering peace. And in a knowledge economy, education is the new currency by which nations maintain economic competitiveness and global prosperity. (2010, p. 4)

Time has thus come to find, build, and use high-quality *visionary* school leadership in its many dimensions; thus, this book takes at least twelve different views (in the chapters) of the visionary roles and functions of education leadership in K–12—building on the roles, theories, and visionary actions of key educators in the schools. No single perspective is enough, as all views must work in concert to the benefit of teachers and students, today. School leaders, moreover, need to have their own vision about the following: (1) what their work entails, (2) how their school should be and look like, and (3) what their staff and students (and schools) can achieve.

For as Debbie Zmorenski explains so well in her general description of leadership in "Why Leaders Must Have Vision" (2016):

> *Great leaders have vision.* However, there are very few natural visionary leaders in the corporate world. I have been lucky to work with two during my 34-year

career with Walt Disney World. The good news is that this is a skill that can be learned. It is probably the most powerful tool in a leader's toolbox. So what is a vision? How does it work, and how is it different from a vision statement?

Great leaders use vision as a tool to inspire and motivate, not to dictate. Do not give your employees the steps for achieving the vision, but let them determine their methods and tactics for achieving the goal. Great leaders know how to give the gift of vision and then step away. (p. 1)

And in many cases, having a vision in leadership also involves taking the right steps carefully at the right time, one by one, to make things work. For example, here's one formula—and steps—that can work to help using vision for school improvement by George Curios (2016) in his article, "The Principal of Change: Stories of Learning and Leading":

- Believing first and foremost in helping to guide others to find their passion.
- Working with students, parents, and staff and clarifying with them the vision of the school. We believe that through focusing on *building relationships* with all stakeholders first, we can ultimately work to ensure that these same stakeholders can become leaders in our school community. This vision is shown through the Forest Green/Connections for Learning Mind Map that is currently under development.
- Through our Education Planning process, we worked with students, staff, and parents to understand our strengths, along with our areas of growth. This was a collaborative endeavor that was well received by the school community.

Many of these educational leaders have worked hard to include parents, community, and staff in school initiatives that are based on current and future school and community needs through open communication. This effort has included communication through monthly newsletters, as well as using a conversational media through the Forest Green School Blog. John Gabriel and Paul Farmer (2009, p. 11) explain the following:

Developing strong vision and mission statements can help stakeholders in your school to reach such a common understanding. A vision is your school's goal—where you hope to see it in the future. The mission provides an overview of the steps planned to achieve that future. A vision is concise and easy to recall, whereas a mission is lengthier and more explanatory in nature. Your school may also want to establish targets along the way to measure progress toward its vision. We begin this chapter with developing your school's vision, because you need to know where you want to be before you can determine how you plan to get there.

INTRODUCTION TO THE BOOK

The first three chapters of this book define and operationalize the term *visionary leadership in education*, and apply it to staff and schools as an introduction in chapter 1. Mentoring is essential in education, and in most professions, where educators learn and practice their teaching skills with other educators – and thus professionals care and can help each other to grow and improve, to the benefit of students as young learners. Chapter 2 questions, what do visionary leaders accomplish in leading programs for students often using mentoring. And chapter 3 discusses the technical side of organizations and visions. Chapter 4 places leadership, with vision, into the needed area of special education in schools, while Chapter 5 puts leadership squarely in the field of teaching and learning with use of "reflective practice". Thus, this book seeks both to describe and analyze the methods and techniques that leaders with vision can use actually to change and improve schools under their control. This first section explains, details, and applies these "techniques" to schools and districts.

These first three chapters explain the knowledge, skills, and professional dispositions that are essential for educational leadership preparation programs to train graduate students with the competency of developing *school vision*. In so doing, this chapter is subdivided into two sections.

The chapter 1's first section *defines* the essential concepts and principles—or conceptual frameworks—of school vision as a prerequisite knowledge base for *visionary leadership*, and clarifies the meaning of Standard 1 and its corresponding indicators of the Professional Standards for Educational Leaders, 2015:

> *Effective educational leaders develop, advocate, and enact a shared mission, vision, and core values of high-quality education and academic success and well-being of each student.*

Then, this chapter 1's second section *uses* this conceptual framework of visionary leadership to provide examples from the field of exemplary educational leadership programs regarding how Standard 1 and its indicators are fully actualized.

REFERENCES

Curios, George. (2016). The principal of change: Stories of learning and leading. http://georgecouros.ca/blog/

Duncan, Arne. (2010). *The vision of education reform in the United States: Secretary Arne Duncan's remarks to United Nations Educational, Scientific and Cultural*

Organization (UNESCO), Paris, France. Washington, DC: U.S. Department of Education, Archived Information.

Gabriel, John G., & Farmer, Paul C. (2009). *How to help your school thrive without breaking the bank.* Alexandria, VA: Association for Supervision and Curriculum Development, ASCD.

Zmorenski, Debbie. (2016). Why leaders must have vision. http://www.reliableplant.com/Read/29109/leaders-have-vision

Chapter 2

Building a Collaborative Visionary Community

Karen Andronico

INTRODUCTION

As the No Child Left Behind Act (NCLB) (2002) relinquishes its reign to the impending, perhaps less punitive, Every Student Succeeds Act—ESSA (2015), the mission, or purpose, for which all public schools across the nation, remains constant: *all* students will learn at high levels. DuFour and Marzano (2011) claim that "schools are [mandated] to bring *every* student to . . . dramatically higher standards of academic achievement;" and that "no generation in the history of the United States has ever been asked to do that" (p. 5). Although current federal policy may change, the stakes remain high for school reform in the United States.

Mattos (2008) warns, "Never have the demands on our educational system been greater—or the consequences of failure so severe" (p. 13). He predicts that the pathways for students who do not succeed in our educational system will "lead to an adult life of hardship, incarceration, or dependence on the welfare system" (p. 13).

Thus, accountability for school reform falls squarely on the shoulders of school leaders who are impelled to improve students' achievement despite outside factors including poverty, high student mobility rates, racial and ethnic achievement gaps, and students with numerous special needs. With the stakes so high for our students, we see "little room for error" (Mattos, 2008, p. 13).

School leadership stands firm as a key variable in school reform because of its strong link to students' learning (Leithwood & Louis, 2012). Furthermore, DuFour and Marzano (2011) contend, "Principal leadership has a significant and positive relationship with student achievement" (p. 48). As pointed out by DuFour and Marzano (2008), school leaders also have an indirect impact on student achievement since they have a direct influence on the teachers whom they lead.

To inspire teachers to believe that *all* students can and will learn at high levels—despite significant achievement gaps—today's school leaders must become visionaries who can communicate compelling views and directions of successful futures for their schools—as well as develop a blueprint for how they will get there. According to the research, the best strategy for building a visionary, collaborative community is to create the culture of a professional learning community (PLC) (DuFour & Marzano, 2011; Fullan, 2001; Little, 2006; McLaughlin & Talbert, 2001).

Mattos (2008) concurs as he explains: "Becoming a *professional learning community* (PLC) is the most powerful and effective process systematically to change school culture and ensure high levels of learning for all students" (p. 14). The culture of a PLC is characterized by a collective commitment to ensure that *all* students—despite outside factors—learn at higher levels—and to act together to make teaching and learning work.

Thus, visionary school leaders must know how to create professional learning communities for school improvement. As Leithwood and Louis (2012) explain,

> Effective school leadership strengthens a professional learning community—a special environment within which teachers work together to improve their practice and improve student learning . . . professional community . . . is a strong predictor of instructional practices that are strongly connected to student achievement. (p. 25)

Therefore, models of the teacher professional community in schools must be firmly embedded in the schools' culture if they are to be effective in school reform. If teachers blame students for poor results, professional learning communities will not succeed. For, unless school leaders understand how to create and sustain collaborative cultures—including the structures, norms, and protocols that support and maintain the work of teacher teams—a professional learning community could prove to be another failed initiative. Most importantly, a moral imperative to close the learning gap for disadvantaged students must drive all collaborative visionary efforts in a professional learning community.

One of the most powerful structures for teacher collaboration within the professional learning community will be explored in this chapter as a model for sustainable school reform. The data team structure represents a cultural shift from teacher *isolation* to teacher *collaboration* and necessitates visionary and transformational school leadership that changes assumptions, values, and beliefs about teaching and learning.

The call for change often originates from federal, state, and local-city-county mandates for improved student performance; however, reform initiatives must be situated within the context of a positive culture of *internal* accountability, where improved results are driven by a collective commitment to the belief that all children *will* learn despite outside factors—and where trust motivates teachers to experiment and take risks to improve teaching and learning.

This chapter explores the following key questions:

1. Why is a professional learning community the best strategy for school improvement?
2. What is the twenty-first century school leader's role in creating and maintaining the culture of a professional learning community?
3. How do school leaders develop and sustain effective data teams within the culture of the PLC?

STATEMENT OF THE PROBLEM

Never before in the history of public schooling in the United States have American professional educators been called upon to ensure that *all* students master the high cognitive demands of the rigorous common core standards, including those students who have traditionally struggled in school. Students who do not achieve success in school may later be more likely to face incarceration, welfare status, poverty, ill health, and shorter life spans (Mattos, 2008).

In the past, education was not necessary for employment because many "dropouts had ready access to the middle-class because of relatively high paying jobs in manufacturing, construction, and mining" (DuFour & Marzano, 2011, p. 10). However, research shows that the shift from farming and goods-producing industries to a service industry has produced an increase in the need for more postsecondary and even graduate education.

Today, educators are called upon to close racial gaps that exist between white students and black and Latino students, who, on the average, are "two to three years behind white students of the same age . . . and their graduation rates are 20 percent lower" (DuFour & Marzano, 2011, pp. 5–6). Compounding the racial gap is the socioeconomic gap, with students who are eligible for free and reduced lunch scoring approximately two years behind their more affluent counterparts (DuFour & Marzano, 2011, p. 6). If these gaps aren't closed, the personal opportunities and incomes of many Americans will decline over the next decade.

Although some may argue that high school graduation rates are up—and students are scoring better on high-stakes exams—evidence now shows that these gains do not have long-term effects. For example, "more than one-third of American high school graduates who enter college are required to take remedial courses," and the chance that those students will graduate from college is very low (DuFour & Marzano, 2011, p. 9).

Currently, approximately half of the new teachers who enter the teaching force will exit it within five years. Furthermore, Miner reports that teacher turnover costs $7.3 billion a year to replace them; and "more teachers are expected to retire between 2010–2020 since any other decade since World War II" ("Teaching's Revolving Door," 2008–2009).

Miner (2008–2009) warns, "If we want teachers . . . who are in it for the long haul, we need to consider how to create schools that are in themselves centers for the continual learning for everyone [including teachers and leaders] connected to them" ("Teaching's Revolving Door"). For that to happen, school leaders must change the organizational structure of their schools by distributing and sharing leadership across the organization.

Another challenge for failure—to ensure all students learn—is the implementation gap. Some schools call themselves PLCs, when, in reality, they are not. Fernandez and Yoshida (2004) claim that "superficial implementation" of reform initiatives is "not likely to have any positive impact on the learning of teachers and students" (as cited in Wiburg & Brown, 2007, p. 13). Many schools that claim to be PLCs are still struggling because they "failed to align their schools' culture and practices with all the essential PLC characteristics" (Mattos, 2008, p. 14).

THEORETICAL BACKGROUND

Visionary, Transformational, and Shared Instructional Leadership

According to Reeves (2006), visionary leaders articulate a compelling vision and link it to the use of clear standards of action that will accomplish the vision (p. 34). Likewise, transformational leaders mobilize constituents to embrace a shared vision and to work together toward its fruition, fostering trust by building the capacity, collaboration, and commitment needed to create an organization devoted to learning and improved results (Kouzes & Posner, 2007). Both visionary and transformational leaders lift their constituents to higher moral ground in their shared promise for a better future.

Shared instructional leadership plays a role in a PLC culture because principals as "chief instructional leaders will consistently engage with teacher teams in discussions of curriculum, assessment, and instruction as they relate to student performance" (Stronge, Richard, & Catano, 2008, p. 8). DuFour and Marzano (2009) "advocate for a new image" for school leaders as "learning leaders" when they continuously seek out evidence of learning, shifting the discussion with teacher teams from "What was taught?" to "What was learned?" (p. 2).

Cultures of Accountability

Creating and nurturing a culture of internal accountability involve knowing how to engage all stakeholders in a commonly shared mission and vision (DuFour, DuFour, & Eaker, 2008). According to Evans (2008), "in accountability cultures, everyone holds each other accountable for their commitments in a positive and productive manner" (p. 35). Likewise, Connors, Smith, and Hickman (2004) define accountability as a "personal choice to rise above one's circumstances and demonstrate the ownership necessary to achieving desired results" (p. 47).

Shared or Distributive Leadership

Kouzes and Posner (2003) claim that "leadership is not a solo act; it's a team performance" (p. 27). DuFour and Marzano (2011) argue that "no single person has all the knowledge, skills, and talent to . . . improve a school, or meet all the needs of every child in his or her classroom" (p. 2). The researchers contend that visionary leaders will not attempt to do it alone; instead they will distribute leadership widely throughout their schools, cultivating a culture of collaboration and commitment to fulfilling the shared vision. DuFour and Marzano (2011) concur: "It will take a collaborative effort and widely dispersed leadership to meet the challenges confronting our schools" (p. 2).

TEACHER COLLABORATION: THE "MISSING LINK" IN SCHOOL REFORM

According to Leana (2011), teacher collaboration is "the missing link in school reform." Elevating "social capital," above other factors related to student achievement such as individual teacher skill, outside consultants, and the principal as the instructional leader, she claims that "the relationships among teachers . . . for improving public schools" has been widely overlooked as the major key in quality school improvement" (p. 2).

Fullan (2008) concurs, explaining that "collaborative cultures generate greater student learning" (p. 8). McLaughlin and Talbert (2001) found that teachers in collaborative cultures take "collective responsibility for all student learning" (p. 139). In these cultures, where "professional interdependence, experimentation, and reflection . . . were the norms . . . student success is explicitly everyone's responsibility" (pp. 51–52). Moreover, teachers in collaborative communities placed their students "at the center" and "adapt their practices to accommodate students," embracing the assumption that it was their responsibility that all students learned (p. 56).

THE CULTURE OF A PROFESSIONAL LEARNING COMMUNITY

The primary purpose of a school PLC is *learning for all students*. DuFour et al. (2006) state, "A PLC is composed of collaborative teams whose members work interdependently to achieve common goals linked to the purpose of learning for all" (p. 3). Thus, leaders, teachers, and students all assume the role of learners in a PLC.

Three "big ideas" drive the work of a PLC. The first and most important tenet is that "the fundamental purpose of school is to ensure that all students *learn*, rather than to see to it that all students are *taught*" (DuFour et al., 2010, p. 7). Thus, it is incumbent on all school leaders to create the culture of a PLC where the expectation is that the school will create systems and structures to ensure that every student learns at high levels. In a PLC, *learning* is the constant, and *time* and *support* become the variables to address student needs.

The second big idea of a PLC is that collaborative culture is necessary to achieve a PLC's purpose. In a PLC, teachers are organized into teams and are expected to work "*interdependently* to achieve common goals for which members were held *mutually accountable*" (DuFour et al., 2010, p. 181).

The third big idea of a *professional learning community* is a constant focus on results. Collaborative teams in a PLC use results of common assessments to monitor students' learning and intervene in a timely manner when students show that they are not progressing.

Six questions guide the work of PLC teams to ensure learning for all:

1. What do we want our students to know? (Curriculum and standards)
2. How will we know our students are learning? (Assessment)
3. How will we respond when students do not learn? (Instruction)
4. How will we enrich and extend the learning for students who are proficient?
5. How will we increase our instructional competence? (Teacher development)
6. How will we coordinate our efforts as a school? (Leadership) (Marzano et al., 2016).

In addition to the three "big ideas," and six guiding questions, six essential elements characterize the culture of a PLC: (1) common mission, vision, values, and goals; (2) collaborative culture; (3) collective inquiry; (4) action orientation; (5) continuous improvement; and (6) focus on results (Mattos, 2008, p. 14). If school leaders neglect or fail to implement deeply any one of these elements, the PLC will fail.

THE LEADER'S ROLE IN BUILDING AND SUSTAINING THE CULTURE OF A PLC

DuFour & Marzano (2009) argues that without the principal's leadership, "the transformation from a culture of isolation to a culture of collaboration" will often not occur (p. 63). Therefore, the role of the school leader in developing and sustaining the culture of professional learning communities is paramount to their success.

Once a school leader has decided that the best strategy for school improvement is a PLC, he or she must understand this role in the deep implementation of the cultural shifts as well as the structures and processes necessary for a PLC to grow and flourish. The PLC is not a new program but an ongoing process for "how we do things here"—and the school leader must know and understand how to lead for successful implementation.

Furthermore, DuFour (2007) stresses the importance of clarity in creating an effective PLC. The visionary PLC leader must be clear on the "fundamental purpose of the organization, the future it must create to better fulfill that purpose, the most high-leverage strategies for creating that future, the indicators of progress it will monitor and the specific ways each member of the organization can contribute both to its long term purpose and short term goals" (2007, p. 41).

According to DuFour et al. (2006), "When a school moves from traditional practice to create a PLC, it undergoes a seismic cultural shift" (p. 186). In a PLC, everyone's role changes: people who worked in isolation will now be asked to work collaboratively; people who held authority will now be asked to share it; but, most importantly, people who acted under certain beliefs and assumptions will be asked to change them.

The PLC leader does this by linking the proposed change to the school's mission, or moral purpose. He or she must illustrate, through the use of relevant data and evidence, that the school's current practices are not working toward meeting their purpose, and then must clearly explain how the change will help the school achieve its primary purpose of ensuring high levels of learning for all students.

Furthermore, DuFour & Marzano (2009) strongly suggest that visionary PLC leaders should "repeatedly address the idea of 'who we are and who we are becoming'" (p. 193). But articulating a vision will fall flat if the actions of the PLC leader do not match his or her words. For example, if a commitment of a PLC is continuous learning for students and adults, then the PLC leader must become the "lead learner."

According to DuFour (2007), leaders who create cultures of internal accountability for sustained improvement are not "laissez-faire" in their leadership approach (p. 39). Rather, they foster autonomy and creativity (loose) within a "systematic framework that stipulates clear non-discretionary priorities and parameters (tight)" (p. 39). For example, collaboratively analyzing data from common assessments is not something teacher teams can opt out of; however, deciding which strategy might have the greatest impact on addressing students' learning gaps as evidenced by that data, is determined by the team.

PLC leaders must not ever compromise the core concepts of the PLC, or they risk its extinction. DuFour et al. (2006) warn, "the most common demise of PLC initiatives is not the result of a single cataclysmic event, but rather repeated compromises regarding the fundamental premises of PLCs. PLCs die from a thousand small wounds" (p. 195).

For example, a teacher may want to forego team meetings based on the argument that she is already getting good results. But teacher collaboration centered on student learning and teacher practice is a nonnegotiable of the PLC. If this teacher is getting good results, her practice needs to be made transparent to the other teachers so that they can improve their practice as well.

DuFour (2007) argues that if PLC leaders' attempts at engaging stakeholders fail, then the leaders should "exercise their authority to require the work be done" asserting that professionals do not have the right to ignore the research on what has been "regarded as best practice in the field" (p. 42).

The next leadership step in making the vision a reality is to build a "guiding coalition" or leadership team to "ensure that there is a critical mass of people willing to move forward and then to push forward despite the objections of those who are not in favor of doing so" (DuFour et al., 2006, p. 197).

DuFour et al. (2006) claim that "one of a leader's highest duties is to foster people's self-efficacy": the belief in themselves that they can play an important part in making the school's vision of a successful future a reality (p. 195). PLC leaders must constantly ignite hope in their schools through their words and actions about their belief that their constituents can accomplish great things through their collective efforts.

COLLABORATIVE TEAMS IN A PLC

In a PLC, teachers meet in teams whose members hold each other collectively responsible for student learning. Whether it is a content team, grade-level team, or vertical team, teams focus on analyzing student data to improve student performance by improving teacher practices.

DuFour and Marzano (2011) claim that because of the emphasis on teacher collaboration and de-privatization of practice rather than teacher isolation, PLC leaders should focus on supporting collaborative teams rather than on supporting individual teachers. DuFour and Marzano (2011) argue, "The principal of a K–5 building can now work closely with six teams rather than thirty individuals . . . and the principal of a large high school can influence twenty team leaders directly rather than 150 teachers indirectly" (p. 51). Therefore, the PLC team provides a vehicle through which the PLC leader can provide support and feedback efficiently.

DuFour and Marzano (2011) contend that "shifting the focus of principals from supervising individual teachers into better performance to helping build the capacity of educators to work as members of results-oriented collaborative teams is perhaps the most powerful strategy" for improving both teaching and learning (p. 62). They claim that research supports the theory that "focusing on individual development does not develop the interdependence, collaboration, and collective effort essential to improving results" (p. 66). Furthermore, closing learning gaps takes more than the skill of individual outstanding teachers but necessitates the building of a collective capacity throughout the school organization.

DuFour and Marzano (2009) assert that the "principal evaluation of teachers is a low-leverage strategy for improving schools" (p. 4). Moreover, evaluation systems that focus mainly on individual, top-down evaluations, where teachers continue to be sorted into "effective and "ineffective" categories, may encourage a feeling of competition and loneliness amongst teachers that could potentially result in toxic cultures where teacher collaboration and teamwork to improve teaching and learning could become of lesser value than individual evaluation ratings.

In addition, the collaborative team structure in a PLC assists the school leader in sharing leadership throughout the organization. According to DuFour and Marzano (2011), effective leaders "foster shared leadership by identifying and developing educators to lead their collaborative teams because without effective leadership at the team level, the collaborative process is likely to drift away from the issues most critical to student learning" (p. 57).

During the team meetings, teachers make clear the essential standards, concepts, and skills to be taught for each unit of study, monitor each student's progress toward mastery of those standards, concepts, and skills through careful analysis of team-created common assessments, and use the data from the common assessments to "inform and improve" their practice.

Without the powerful leadership, teachers will not work productively in teams. As DuFour and Marzano (2011) claim, "Collaborating on the wrong work and engaging in collective inquiry into the wrong questions will not have an impact on student achievement" (p. 79).

To build the capacity of individual teachers as members of powerful, results-driven teams, a principal or school leader would engage in the following actions:

1. Design schedules to guarantee that teams meet minimally one hour per week during the school day.
2. Provide teams with the support, training, resources, tools, templates, norms, and training they need to be productive in the team structure.
3. Ensure consistent delivery of curriculum across the grades; provide resources for curriculum development; support teachers in the identification of the common essential standards, content, skills, and concepts to be taught.
4. Build shared knowledge on best assessment practices and train them how to create common assessments and rubrics to assist them in focusing on learning.
5. And ask the team to reflect on the following questions to help keep a laser-like focus on learning with these questions:

   - How will our team monitor the learning of each student on a timely basis?
   - Do our common assessments reflect the characteristics of quality assessments that we have identified?
   - How are we using the results from assessments to support students who are experiencing difficulty?
   - What criteria are the members of your team using to assess the quality of students' work?
   - What evidence do you have that members of your team apply the criteria consistently? (DuFour & Marzano, 2009, p. 6)

DATA TEAMS: A MODEL FOR TEACHER COLLABORATION

Instructional data teams (IDTs) offer a powerful structure for teacher collaboration within a PLC culture. Within this model, teachers collectively learn to use "more effective researched-based practices . . . and learn to strengthen the connection between teacher actions and student performance" (McNulty & Besser, 2010, p. 23).

Simply put, "an Instructional Data Team is a small grade-level, department, course-alike, or organizational team that examines work generated from common assessment" (Peery, 2011, p. 1). A common assessment, usually created by the team, focuses on the "prioritized standards" or course outcomes, and "serves as the basis for the discussion of changes in instructional practice" (Peery, 2011, p. 2).

During meetings, data teams focus on the impact of their instruction on student learning. Any issues that do not focus around teaching and learning are discussed at other times. On average, data teams meet twice monthly for 60–90 minutes, but meeting once weekly would be optimal.

Data team members follow the six-step data team process in cycles of continuous improvement:

1. *Collect and chart/display the data*: Team members record the number and percentage of students who scored proficient and nonproficient on the pre-common assessment. They identify students by name who are proficient or above, close to proficient, approaching proficient, and struggling students.
2. *Analyze data and prioritize needs*: Team members examine the common assessment results and look for patterns and trends of student strengths and learning gaps and prioritize needs. They make inferences as to why the students are performing the way they are. They match student-learning needs with research-based instructional strategies.
3. *Set, review, and revise incremental SMART goals*: The team members set a SMART goal (Strategic, Measureable, Achievable, Relevant, and Timely) for improved results on the post-common assessment.
4. *Select common instructional strategies*: The team members choose the common instructional strategies to be employed to address the learning challenges discovered in step 2. The team members will implement one or two research-based instructional strategies to address the learning gap that was identified during the analysis of the pre-common assessment. Team members should model the strategy for one another so they can agree upon how the strategy will be implemented.
5. *Determine results indicators*: Team members describe the behavior and actions of teachers and students and other evidence to determine if the intervention strategy is implemented correctly.
6. *Evaluate and monitor results*: During this step, team members monitor the effectiveness of the implementation of the research-based strategy through peer observation and looking at student work samples collected between the pre- and post-common assessments (Peery, 2011, p. 3).

DATA TEAM CONFIGURATIONS

Data teams may be organized in several ways but must have a common assessment to make the work of the team purposeful. The following data team configurations can be used successfully:

1. *Horizontal teams* consist of an entire grade level.
2. *Vertical teams* consist of teachers from several grade levels. For example, in a middle school, a vertical team may consist of teachers from grades 6, 7, and 8.

3. *Specialist teams* focus on a "special need that students have demonstrated." (Peery, 2011, p. 11)

DATA TEAM ROLES

To ensure the effective functioning of data teams, specific roles are assigned to its members. The data team leader has the most important role because he or she communicates the assumption to the other members that all students can achieve at high levels and will challenge those team members who might blame the students for their lack of achievement. In addition, the data team leader should be well versed in research-based instructional strategies. The other data team roles include recorder, data technician, data wall curator, timekeeper, and focus monitor (Peery, 2011, p. 14). Other responsibilities of the data team members include active listening; asking probing questions to deepen the team's understanding of their work; sharing and making copies of common assessments, minutes, and data charts; and being invested in learning research-based strategies.

THE ROLE OF THE SCHOOL LEADER IN DATA TEAMS

McNulty and Besser (2010) describe the role of the school leader in developing powerful data teams, explaining that "principals . . . must be the lead advocates for IDT's, because IDT's are a powerful form of professional development and the key to improving teaching, learning, and leadership" (p. 113). McNulty and Besser (2010) claim that the "building principal will drive the success or failure of the IDT process," and they advise school leaders to "capture your success stories, share your journey using your results, and celebrate the deliberate and positive impact that Data Teams have on student learning" (p. 113).

After receiving intensive training in the data team process, bold school leaders must face teacher resistance and seek out those individuals who are ready for change and whose beliefs support the data team process. In this way, the school leader can begin to build a school leadership team and can fill the leadership positions for the data teams.

School leaders provide ongoing feedback to data teams after observing their meetings and reviewing their common assessment data (see Cooper & McCray, 2015, p. 35). According to McNulty and Besser (2010, p. 154), the "most important feedback a leader can provide is on the use of the five-step meeting or the six-step Data Teams process," (Cooper & Gargan, 2009).

In addition to providing feedback to each data team, using a data team rubric, the school leader should meet with each data team at least once per month and review the effectiveness and impact of curriculum units, common assessment data, smart goals, and instructional strategies on student learning. The school leader should also provide feedback on work products the data team has created including meeting agendas, common assessments, unit maps, and data charts from common assessments.

Peery (2011) summarizes the role of the principal in monitoring data teams using the "four Cs":

1. *Clear course*: The school leader clearly communicates the mission and vision for data teams and then provides the required time, resources, scheduling, support, and so on, for them to be successful.
2. *Constant feedback*: School leaders must observe data team meetings and provide feedback to the team for improvement. Additionally, school leaders may provide individual feedback to teachers on effective use of intervention strategies.
3. *Course correction:* Teams must be given time to improve incrementally.
4. *Celebrate success*: School leaders should celebrate data teams' successes, no matter how small. (p. 40)

The monitoring of data teams by school administration sends a strong message regarding the importance of the process. In addition, through the observation process, school leaders can highlight effective teams by videotaping their meeting and showing it to the other teams as a form of professional development.

CONCLUSION

In an era where the stakes remain high for students who struggle in school and face dire consequences if they are not successful, school leaders are impelled to implement deeply professional learning communities that ensure learning for *all* students. Campsen (2010) concludes, "The use of student assessment data to shape and drive the entire instructional program in a school is most effectively done through data teams that operate in an environment of shared leadership with the principal" (p. 133).

This clearly reflects the culture of data-driven accountability and distributed leadership that characterizes a professional learning community. To root deeply both the culture of a professional learning community and the data team process into the existing culture of a school, school leaders must be visionary and transformational. To face opposition and resistance to the change, school leaders for the twenty-first century must be courageous and bold.

REFERENCES

Campsen, L. (2010). Data teams from a principal's perspective. In *Data teams the big picture: Looking at data teams through a collaborative lens*. Englewood, CO: Lead + Learn Press.

Connors, R., & Smith T., Hickman, C. (2004). *The Oz principle: Getting results through individual and organizational accountability*. New York: Penguin.

Cooper, B. S., & Gargan, A. (2009). Rubrics in education: Old term, new meanings. *Phi Delta Kappan* (May/June/July), 54–55.

Cooper, B. S., & McCray, C. D. (2015). *Mentoring for School Quality: Relating Leadership to School Improvement*. Lanham, MD: Rowman & Littlefield.

DuFour, R. (2007, November). In praise of top-down leadership. *The School Administrator, 64*(10), 38–42.

DuFour, R., DuFour, R., & Eaker, R. (2008). *Revisiting professional learning communities at work: New insights for improving schools*. Bloomington, IN: Solution Tree Press.

Du Four, R., DuFour, R., Eaker, R., & Karhanek, G. (2010). *Raising the bar and closing the gap: Whatever it takes*. Bloomington, IN: Solution Tree Press.

DuFour, R., DuFour, R., Eaker, R., & Many, T. (2006). *Learning by doing: A handbook for professional learning communities at work*. Bloomington, IN: Solution Tree Press.

DuFour, R., & Marzano, R. (2009). High leverage strategies for principal leadership. *Educational Leadership, 66*(5), 62–68.

DuFour, R., & Marzano, R. (2011). *Leaders of learning: How district, school, and classroom leaders improve student achievement*. Bloomington, IN: Solution Tree Press.

Evans, H. (2008). *Winning with accountability*. Dallas, TX: Cornerstone Leadership Institute.

Fullan, M. F. (2008). *What's worth fighting for in the principalship*. New York: Teachers College Press.

Kouzes, J., & Posner, B. (2003). Challenge is the opportunity for greatness. *Leader to Leader, 28*, 16–23.

Kouzes, J., & Posner, B. (2007). *The leadership challenge*. San Francisco, CA: Jossey-Bass.

Leana, C. R. (2011, Fall). The missing link in school reform. *Stanford Social Innovation Review*, 30–35.

Leithwood, K., & Louis, K. S. (2012). *Linking leadership to student learning*. San Francisco, CA: Library of Congress.

Little, J. W. (2006). *Professional community and professional development in the learning-centered school*. Washington, DC: National Education Association.

Marzano, R., Heflebower, T., Hoegh, J., Warrick, P., & Grift, G. (2016). *Collaborative teams that transform schools: The next step in PLCs*. [Kindle edition].

Mattos, M. (2008). Walk the "Lign: Aligning school practices with essential PCL characteristics." In *The collaborative administrator: Working together as a professional learning community*. Bloomington, IN: Solution Tree Press.

McLaughlin, M. W., & Talbert, J. E. (2001). *Professional communities and the work of high school teaching.* Chicago: University of Chicago Press.

McNulty, B., & Besser, L. (2010). *Leaders make it happen: An administrator's guide to data teams.* Englewood, CO: Lead + Learn Press.

Miner, B. (2008–2009, Winter). "Teaching's revolving door." *Rethinking Schools.* Retrieved from www.rethinkingschools.org/special_reports/quality_teachers/door232.shtml.

New York State Education Department (2015). *Every student succeeds act.* Retrieved from www.ed.gov/essa?src=rn.

Peery, A. (2011). *The data teams experience: A guide for effective meetings.* Englewood, CO: Lead + Learn Press.

Reeves, D. (2006). *The learning leader.* Alexandria, VA: Association for Curriculum and Supervision.

Stronge, J., Richard, H., & Catano, N. (2008). *Qualities of effective principals.* Alexandria, VA: Association for Curriculum and Supervision. Retrieved from http://www.ascd.org/publications/books/108003/chapters/Instructional-Leadership@-Supporting-Best-Practice.aspx

Wiburg, K., & Brown, S. (2007). *Lesson study.* Thousand Oaks, CA: Corwin Press.

Chapter 3

Visionary School Finance Leadership in a "Capped" Fiscal Environment

Stephen V. Coffin

SETTING

A school district's budget is the financial representation of its educational hopes and plans. The budget demonstrates how financial, material, and human resources will be acquired and allocated to accomplish the educational plan. And the financial plan explains the mix of revenue sources with which the district will acquire the financial, material, and human resources necessary to achieve the educational plans and goals.

The sources of revenue have become increasingly strained. Like many states, property taxes in New Jersey provide the majority of funding for *traditional public school districts* (TPSDs), municipal governments, and county governments. Costs for the public goods and services, especially public education provided by these entities, have increased commensurate with the increasing demand for local public goods and services.

Meeting the increasing demand for locally provided public goods and services—while providing a top quality public education that meets the needs of all students—is increasingly difficult with these three entities increasing local property tax burdens on the same tax base. Similarly, state and federal aid continues to fund less of the cost of their mandates. The increasing amount of underfunded state and federal mandates force TPSDs to make up the shortfall from local sources, particularly property taxes.

Meeting demands for increased revenues from higher property tax levies to offset increased costs is increasingly difficult, using existing tax bases. The valuation of local tax bases—or total ratable properties—is often exceeded by the increased demand for local revenues and the combined local property burden. Assessed values, on which property taxes are levied, yield diminishing marginal returns because the increasing cost of providing local public goods and services—especially public education—have often outstripped increases in assessed property values and taxes.

TAX LEVY CAPS: CREATING THE "TRIPLE WHAMMY"

Tax levy caps often compound the problem of raising revenues to meet the increasing cost of local provided public goods and services—especially education. A tax levy cap or tax—and a *tax expenditure limit* (TEL)—are intended to limit the amount and growth rate of property taxes. In theory, TELs accomplish this goal by forcing TPSDs to prioritize budgets; minimizing waste, inefficiencies, and duplication; and allocating resources commensurate with the prioritization of the programs or services provided. Examples of states with TELs include New Jersey's 2.0 percent cap, Massachusetts's Proposition 2.5, and California's Proposition 13.

Tax levy caps or deeply TELs have fixed percentage point limitations that are imposed on all TPSDs statewide as is New Jersey's 2.0 percent cap. Thus, TELs establish arbitrary one-size-fits-all limits on the amount of property taxes that TPSDs can levy independent of local needs and priorities, and the district's ability to raise revenues. Although waivers on select budgetary growth components are available—if the TPSD meets certain conditions—the one-size-fits-all approach fits no district because school districts have unique needs; varying levels of financial, material, and human resources; and varying property tax-raising capacity.

Moreover, TELs do not account for inflation or the cost of living for a TPSD. Thus, TPSDs face a "triple whammy" of (1) increasingly underfunded state and federal mandates, (2) increasing local property tax burdens approaching a theoretical threshold, and (3) the imposition of tax levy caps or TELs.

LOCAL SCHOOL DISTRICT, NOT COUNTY PROPERTY TAXES, ARE INVESTED IN HOST MUNICIPALITY

All of a local school district's property taxes are invested and remain in the schools of the host municipality, so that the taxpayers benefit more fully from the property taxes levied and collected. County property taxes differ sharply from those levied to fund our public schools because they are not fully invested in the host community. New Jersey county property taxes, for example, are redistributed to support an unaccountable, wasteful, and duplicative layer of government. In fact, no program or service is offered at the county level that is not already offered at the state or local level. These factors demonstrate that county government is duplicative and wasteful; and

Connecticut eliminated county government in 1960, when the state had no state income or sales tax.

When New Jersey implemented its 2.0 percent TEL or cap, taxpayers could vote on their local school district budgets in all but a handful of towns; districts now vote on the budget only if the budget exceeds the TEL or cap. However, no taxpayer is able to vote on the budget of his/her municipal or county government despite that these two levels of government are funded almost entirely by local property taxes. Because taxpayers can vote on school budgets, they can hold their school systems accountable.

However, without a vote on municipal and county government budgets, taxpayers are limited in their ability to hold these levels of government accountable. This situation is one of the chief reasons why statewide county government costs New Jersey's taxpayers more than $8.0 billion annually!

NECESSARY RELIANCE ON PROPERTY TAXES

To fund its budget properly, a TPSD must have the ability to raise the revenues commensurate with meeting the goals expressed in its unique educational needs and plan (O'Sullivan, Sexton, & Sheffrin, 2007). Every district's budget is unique because educational resource requirements, student needs, and per pupil cost to educate vary by district. The fact that funding our public schools largely through local property taxes is essential caused O'Sullivan, Sexton, & Sheffrin (2007) to conclude:

> The property tax can be administered by local government with relatively little fear of its tax base migrating to other jurisdictions, thus providing local governments with the needed fiscal autonomy. The property tax has been the source of economic independence of local units of government. (p. 94)

Property taxes provide local public school districts with a predictable, reliable, and sustainable sources of revenue for a given tax base that are "consistent with both the ability-to-pay principle and the benefit principle of taxation" (O'Sullivan et al., 2007, p. 15).

TELs PLUS UNDERFUNDED STATE AND FEDERAL MANDATES CAUSE CUTS TO REGULAR EDUCATION FUNDING

Only two kinds of programs and services are offered by TPSDs: those that are mandate-protected and those that are not mandate-protected. Because school districts are forced by state and federal governments to fund the unfunded portion of their mandates, TDSDs are forced to cut non–mandate-protected programs and services while budgeting within the 2.0 percent tax levy cap and offsetting inflation. However, TPSDs often have little or no control over many of such major cost drivers in the incremental expenditures resulting from increases in underfunded mandates, enrollment, utilities, transportation, health insurance, legal actions, and the number as well as the mix of special education students.

Hence, a TEL may force a typical school district to take alternative actions. One such alternative action taken by typical TPSDs in response to a *tax expenditure limit* is to increase class size to reduce school costs. Increased class size minimizes expenditures for teachers and aides—and other materials and supplies for the kids in the classroom. But larger class sizes may lead to less learning—and lower test scores. Thus, TELs often force TPSDs to cut spending in regular education programs and services to stay within the cap.

NO SUCH THING AS A FREE LUNCH

Proponents of TELs purport that TPSDs will be become more financially responsible because of the state imposed limit on their expenditures and tax levies. TEL supporters also argue that if school districts are left to their own devices, they would continue to spend and tax at ever increasing rates—while the TEL's implementation will force school districts to hold down expenditures and property taxes. TEL advocates seem to expect public school districts to provide the same level of public goods and services—if not a higher quality of education—but at a lower price.

TEL proponents and policymakers disaffected by the seemingly ever-increasing size and cost of public education assert that TELs will lower property taxes and make the provision of public education more efficient, rather than cutting essential educational programs and services.

Although many policymakers realize there is no such thing as a "free lunch," TEL advocates claim that school systems could provide at least the same quantity of education without lowering the quality of education because the TEL would compel districts to eliminate waste. But no TEL can guarantee that any school district will not cut non–mandate-protected programs and services—or regular education—before eliminating any waste or inefficiency.

The passage of the major TELs, such as Proposition 2.5 in Massachusetts and Proposition 13 in California, shows how frustrated voters resorted to a cap that they perceived as the best means available to remedy their situations. Voters seemed to believe prior to the vote that the imposition of the TEL would substantially eliminate inefficiency, waste, and overspending—but it would do so without lowering the quality or quantity of public goods and services such as public education.

However, once the TELs were imposed in Massachusetts and California, many taxpayers acted "consistent with a regret theory of tax limits" (O'Sullivan, 2001, p. 196).

The history of TELs, budgetary caps, or wage and price controls—such as those imposed under former president Nixon—demonstrates that placing arbitrary limits on revenues and expenditures results in a corresponding reduction in the quantity and quality of the public programs and services provided by the TEL-affected entity.

Thus, Downes and Figlio (2008) concluded that TPSD proponents who assert that "constitutional constraints like Proposition 13 could reduce the size of local governments and, at the same time, have little or no effect on the quality of public services provided" – such as seeking a "free lunch" (p. 384). TELs level down the quality of education proportional to the extent a district is TEL-affected.

APPLES VERSUS ORANGES: MASSACHUSETTS'S PROPOSITION 2.5 VERSUS NEW JERSEY'S 2.0 PERCENT CAP

Unlike New Jersey's 2.0 percent cap, Massachusetts imposed its 2.5 percent tax expenditure limit during an economic boom and provided significant amounts of incremental state aid to school districts to make up for the loss of local property tax revenue. However, New Jersey's economic recession—with its concomitant state budget deficits—resulted in cuts to state educational aid. The outlook for New Jersey's TPSDs is grim.

State aid continues to decline—or remain flat—despite changing budgetary requirements and varying student educational needs. Little or no incremental state financial aid seems forthcoming to offset increases in per pupil cost to educate that exceed increases in property tax revenues. These factors most likely will force New Jersey TPSDs to continue to cut non–mandate-protected educational programs and services more deeply than was experienced in Massachusetts.

State aid is unreliable. Massachusetts's educational aid fluctuates, while California has not complied with Proposition 98's constitutional guarantees to provide state aid to local school districts to make up for the property tax revenues lost under Proposition 13. As a result of Proposition 13, California's per pupil spending fell precipitously to an average of approximately $7,500 per pupil—as compared to an average of $47,000 per inmate at its state penal institutions—while its average class sizes became the second highest in the nation.

Also, Massachusetts imposed its 2.5 percent cap during a period of declining student enrollment, while New Jersey's student enrollment levels continue to increase. Massachusetts's lower school district expenditures were largely offset by a much lower level of student enrollment that helped to greatly minimize the cuts to educational programs and services unlike New Jersey.

TAXPAYERS' EXPECTATIONS FOR A TEL

Taxpayers may tend to believe that tax expenditure limits will force greater accountability, efficiency, and transparency, which will lead to lower spending and property taxes. However, voters do not want fewer public goods and services. Voters desire a lower price for the public goods and services that they enjoy—and from which they benefit, especially public education. Taxpayers may sense that TPSDs overtax because of inefficiencies.

However, New Jersey's 2.0 percent TEL lacks the flexibility for municipal governments and TPSDs to respond appropriately to unforeseen adverse circumstances—or a declining economy. For instance, public schools tend to experience an increase of students transferring from private schools when the economy declines as parents become increasingly challenged to find ways to pay for tuition in addition to property taxes. New Jersey's 2.0 percent cap cannot guarantee that any level of government will operate at peak efficiency before cutting the public goods and services including education that they provide. The TEL's limitations restrict the flexibility of school districts' budgetary and property tax policies to meet changing budgetary requirements and varying levels of students' educational needs.

TELs' IMPACT ON EDUCATION AND STUDENT ACHIEVEMENT

Tax levy caps may not only limit the amount of property tax revenue available to school districts but also adversely affect the provision of educational programs and services, and student performance. TELs often result in larger class sizes that adversely affect students' test scores particularly in urban areas (Downes, Dye, & McGuire, 1998; Downes & Figlio, 1999a, 1999b; Figlio, 1997). When it comes to education, TELs can lead to a reduction in quantity as well as quality, and a leveling down of student achievement.

TELs seem adversely to affect students' achievement disproportionately to the amount of property tax revenues lost or expenditures cut. Downes and Figlio (2008) conclude that TPSDs "lead to reductions in student outcomes that are far larger than might be expected given the changes in spending"

(p. 374). Possible explanations for this result include disproportionate cuts in instructional rather than administrative expenditures, higher student-teacher ratios, and a moving perhaps of the more talented or high-scoring test students to private or charter schools.

Because teacher salaries and benefits generally account for more than approximately 70 percent of a typical TPSD's budget, it stands to reason that these expenses would be cut significantly. Reductions of teachers under the constraints of a TEL often lead to larger class sizes which—when combined with the loss of regular educational programs and services—tend to result in the transfer of many students, especially the more gifted ones, to private schools (Downes & Figlio, 2008).

LEVELING DOWN THE QUALITY OF PUBLIC EDUCATION

Although New Jersey's TEL aims to reduce local public school districts' property tax increases to no more than 2.0 percent annually, the cap most likely contributes to a leveling-down of the quality of public education. Our nation's two major TELs—California's Proposition 13 and Massachusetts's Proposition 2.5—on which New Jersey's TEL is modeled, demonstrate the downside of such caps.

These TELs severed the connection among local control, property taxes, school district budgets, educational quality, and taxpayer support because taxpayers lost their ability to hold local school districts accountable while maximizing property values (Fischel, 2001).

New Jersey's 2.0 percent TEL is a one-size-fits-all approach for education—but one that fits no district. As Baker, Green, and Richards (2008) explain, "The local property tax empowers local voters to express what they want for their local public schools" (p. 66). But when statewide TEL imposes artificial budgetary constraints, local control of school district budgets is lost. Thus, the TEL leads to many school district budgets that are incongruous with the needs, size, and priorities of local school districts.

TAXPAYERS' LOWERED SENSE OF OWNERSHIP OF THEIR LOCAL SCHOOLS

Restrictions on property tax revenues through the 2.0 percent TEL reduce the level of local investment in the school district, for the ownership stake held by local taxpayers is similarly reduced. Fischel (2001) explains this concept using the preferences of taxpayers without children in the local public schools, "At the local level, they are willing to support, or at least not oppose, high levels of spending because better schools add to the value of their homes" (p. 152).

However, "At the state level, voters without children do not perceive such an offsetting benefit to their taxes" following the imposition of a statewide TEL (Fischel, 2001, p. 152). The imposition of a TEL reduces local control with a corresponding drop in the level of accountability required by local stakeholders and, therefore, local public school quality often declines.

SCHOOL CHOICE BY "VOTING WITH YOUR FEET"

Taxpayers choose the local public school district that best meets their needs and one that will contribute to their property values by exercising Tieboutian school choice and voting with their feet in selecting a place to live (Tiebout, 1956). But taxpayers vote not only with their feet but also based on local school district's operating budgets, capital projects, and board of education members. Through the exercise of these votes, taxpayers can often control the quality of education provided by their local schools, as well as the level of property taxes levied. Their collective decisions can lead to a Pareto-efficient allocation of local public education.

However, a TEL, such as New Jersey's 2.0 percent tax levy cap, disrupts the equilibrium enjoyed by local public school districts (Tiebout, 1956). The cap does so by artificially limiting budgets, sometimes below the levels congruent with the needs and priorities of local school districts.

TEL restraints cause local school districts to become increasingly challenged to meet student, school, and taxpayer needs. Because the quality of a taxpayer's local public schools is capitalized in the value of his/her home, New Jersey's 2.0 percent TEL most likely not only levels down the quality of locally provided public education but also the property values in districts disproportionately affected by the TEL.

REFERENCES

Baker, B. D., Green, P., & Richards, C. E. (2008). *Financing education systems.* Upper Saddle River, NJ: Pearson Education, Inc.

Downes, T. A., Dye, R. F., & McGuire, T. J. (1998). Do limits matter? Evidence on the effects of tax limitations on student performance." *Journal of Urban Economics, 43,* 401–417.

Downes, T. A., & Figlio, D. N. (1999a). Do tax and expenditure limits provide a free lunch? Evidence on the link between limits and public sector service quality. *National Tax Journal, 52,* 113–128.

Downes, T. A., & Figlio, D. N. (1999b). Economic inequality and the provision of schooling. *Federal Reserve Bank of New York, Economic Policy Review, 5*, 99–110.

Downes, T. A., & Figlio, D. N. (2008). Tax and expenditure limits, school finance and school quality. In H. F. Ladd & E. B. Fiske (Eds.), *The handbook of research in education finance and policy* (pp. 373–388). New York: Routledge Taylor & Francis Group.

Figlio, D. N. (1997). Did the "tax revolt" reduce school performance? *Journal of Public Economics, 65*, 245–269.

Fischel, W. (2001). *The home-voter hypothesis: How home values influence local government taxation, school finance, and land-use policies*, Cambridge, MA: Harvard University Press.

O'Sullivan, A., (2001). Limits on local property taxation: The United States experience. In Oates, W. E., (Ed.), *Property taxation and local government finance* (pp. 177–200). Cambridge, MA: Lincoln Institute of Land Policy.

O'Sullivan, A., Sexton, T. A., & Sheffrin, S. M. (2007). *Property taxes and tax revolts: The legacy of Proposition 13*. Cambridge, MA: Cambridge University Press.

Tiebout, C. M., (1956). A pure theory of local expenditures. *Journal of Political Economy, 64*, 416–424.

Chapter 4

Visionary School Leaders for the Twenty-First Century in Special Education

Su-Je Cho, Kwang-Sun Cho Blair, and Holly Rittenhouse-Cea

Since the *Individuals with Disabilities Education Act* (IDEA) was first promulgated in 1975, substantial changes have occurred in educating students with disabilities. One of the most significant developments is the inclusion of students with disabilities in general education. The 36th Annual Report to Congress showed that students aged six through twenty-one served under IDEA, Part B were educated in regular classrooms (U.S. Department of Education, 2014).

The report further shows that while approximately 95 percent of these students were in regular classrooms for some portion of the day, over 60 percent were in the regular classroom 80 percent or more of the day (U.S. Department of Education, 2014). The federal laws, IDEA, and the *Every Student Succeeds Act* (ESSA, signed in 2015) provide strong support for inclusion practices and recognize that inclusion is highly relevant to the needs of *all* students.

However, achievement outcomes and post–secondary school success for these students have been reported as far below desirable levels (Feng & Sass, 2012). As related to these negative outcomes, great variability exists among schools, districts, and states in regard to how to define inclusion and how it is practiced. As such, general education teachers have negative perceptions about students with disabilities and have difficulty working with these students (Lopes, Monteiro, & Sil, 2004; Santoli et al., 2008). Emphasis on compliance and procedures to accountability for educational outcomes for students with disabilities has created great challenges for school leaders (Burdette, 2010).

In this chapter, we will describe three critical impetuses that will significantly impact the school in regard to inclusion practices for the upcoming years. These features include (1) the reauthorized federal education laws that apply to educating students with disabilities, (2) the framework of school-wide positive behavioral interventions and supports (SWPBIS), and (3) the preparation of students with disabilities for online learning environments. We shall further describe effective strategies and suggestions for visionary leaders to plan and implement these features to improve educational, behavioral, and social-emotional outcomes for students with disabilities.

LAWS THAT PROTECT EDUCATIONAL RIGHTS TO STUDENTS WITH DISABILITIES

Every Student Succeeds Act

The United States Congress reauthorized the fifty-year-old *Elementary and Secondary Education Act* (ESEA, 2015). In December 2015, President Obama signed the *Every Student Succeeds Act* (ESSA), the new name of the *No Child Left Behind* (NCLB). As the federal education law, the ESSA eliminated much of the prescriptiveness of the NCLB. In addition, it sets high standards and contains policies that will help schools prepare *all* students for success in college and future careers (Michigan School Business Officials, 2016).

The ESSA is expected to reduce federal intervention in state education policymaking and to allow states more authority to create their own accountability systems (PSEA Education Services Division, 2016). The law also establishes educational rights of students with disabilities to some extent. Alvarez (2016) summarized some key provisions of the act that apply to educating students with special needs:

1. ESSA requires disaggregating data by student subgroups, including students with disabilities as defined under IDEA.
2. The Act recognizes that the Individualized Education Program (IEP) team is in the best position to make essential decisions about the academic, behavioral, social, and emotional needs of students with disabilities.
3. The Act includes Specialized Instructional Support Personnel (SISP) in a more intentional and strategic way. In addition to working with students with disabilities, SISP can implement early intervention programs to help identify students who need specific and intensive supports. SISP can further help those in a special education setting transition into a general education classroom.
4. The Act ensures that students with disabilities identified under IDEA—and those who receive accommodations under other acts (such as Section 504)—have access to appropriate accommodations.
5. The Act places 1 percent of all students for taking alternative assessments aligned to alternative academic achievement standards for students with

the most significant cognitive disabilities. States are required to monitor local educational agencies (LEAs) that put a number of students in alternative assessment plans.
6. The Act acknowledges the right of parents and guardians to opt their children out of statewide academic assessments where state or local policies allow them to do so.

Guidance to transitioning to the ESSA was specifically described in the document, entitled *Transitioning to the Every Student Succeeds Act (ESSA): Frequently Asked Questions* (U.S. Department of Education, June 2016). School leaders should use this document to be familiar with and implement ESSA at their school. In addition, they should respond to the ESSA state plan.

REAUTHORIZATION OF THE *INDIVIDUALS WITH DISABILITIES EDUCATION ACT*

In late 2016, Congress began to prepare the reauthorization of IDEA. Council for Exceptional Children (CEC), one of the most influential organizations in special education, put together recommendations for Congress to consider during reauthorization. Some key recommended items are (1) parental right to revoke consent for special education and related services, (2) representation of parents and schools by non-attorneys in due process hearings, (3) allocation of federal funds, (4) benchmarks and short-term objectives included in the IEP, and (5) inappropriate use of restraints and seclusion techniques. The rationale and explanations for each recommended item are described in the following (CEC, n.d.).

First, the current IDEA regulations specify that a parent may revoke consent for special education and related services. The regulations also require the school district to comply with the parent's request for their child to be removed from special education. This regulation ensures that schools will not challenge a parent's decision that they made for their child (Pacer Center, 2010). CEC opposes this regulation for two reasons.

First, this regulation relieves LEAs of the responsibility to provide free appropriate public education (FAPE) and develop an IEP for students with disabilities. Instead of relieving the responsibility, CEC posits that the regulation should permit the LEA to pursue a due process hearing or mediation to make efforts to override a parent's decision to revoke consent.

Second, the IDEA states that schools and parents may utilize non-attorneys in due process hearing if a state puts laws prohibiting it in place (Pacer Center, 2010). The U.S. Department of Education (2008) acknowledges that regarding the representational role of non-attorneys in due process hearings;

and the issue of whether non-attorneys may "represent" parties to a due process hearing is a matter that is left to each state to decide according to IDEA (Fed. Reg. at 73006). The current regulations can create a problem for parents or LEAs (CEC, n.d.).

Third, allocation of federal funds in special education has also been an ongoing issue. Over the past several years, near-flat funding for IDEA State Grants has been provided (CEC, n.d.). As such, the formula used to distribute federal funding to the states is outdated (McCann, 2014). The existing federal formula is so distorted that a few states disproportionately benefit at the expense of states more in need of federal special education dollars (McCann, 2014).

To make it worse, IDEA 2004 mandated allocation of Part B funds to LEAs that are not serving students with disabilities. This regulation has resulted in taking limited federal funds from LEAs and giving it to public charter or other types of schools that do not serve children with disabilities (CEC, n.d.).

Fourth, IDEA 2004 eliminated benchmarks and short-term objectives from the IEP for students with disabilities, except those who are eligible to take state alternative assessments. Eliminating these "critical" elements is a problem because the annual goals are not as specific and measurable as benchmarks and short-term objectives.

With this change, teachers have difficulty evaluating whether a student with a disability is making expected progress toward the annual goals. When benchmarks and short-term objectives are specifically written, teachers can use them as a roadmap and a clear mechanism to evaluate the student's annual goals in the IEP (Wrightslaw, 2016). Therefore, it is a state's discretionary decision to use benchmarks and short-term objectives with other students with disabilities. As the U.S. Department of Education (2006) states:

> Benchmarks and short-term objectives were specifically removed from the Act. However, because benchmarks and short-term objectives were originally intended to assist parents in monitoring their child's progress toward meeting the child's annual goals, we believe a State could, if it chose to do so, determine the extent to which short-term objectives and benchmarks would be used. (71, Fed. Reg. at 46663)

Fifth, IDEA permits public schools to use physical restraint and seclusion although the Act discourages their use to the greatest extent possible. The use of restraint and seclusion in many schools has had negative consequences. Nationally, more than 2.8 million K–12 students received one or more out-of-school suspensions during the 2014–2015 academic year (U.S. Department of Education, 2016).

Similarly, many schools use corporal punishment to discipline student misbehavior; it is still a legal form of school discipline in twenty-two states, as of March 2016 (U.S. Department of Education, 2016). During the 2013–2014 academic year, over 110,000 students were subject to corporal punishment in school (U.S. Department of Education, 2015).

The academic performance of schools in states where corporal punishment is widely used was worse than those in states that prohibit corporal punishment (Hickman, 2008). The majority of suspensions, expulsions, and corporal punishments resulted from minor offenses such as infractions of school rules, bus misbehavior, cell phone use, and inappropriate language (Gershoff & Font, 2016; Fabelo et al., 2011). However, IDEA gives schools the power to change placements unilaterally if a student with a disability violates the code of conduct in the school (H.R. 1350).

This effect would give incentives for LEAs to change the student's placement for the school's own convenience (Wrightslaw, 2006). Organizations (e.g., CEC [Council for Exception Children], National School Boards Association, 1922) urged Congress to enact a law that prohibits the inappropriate use of seclusion and restraint as a part of reauthorization efforts. No evidence supports that using restraint or seclusion is effective in reducing the rates of problem behaviors.

SCHOOL-WIDE POSITIVE BEHAVIORAL INTERVENTIONS AND SUPPORTS

School-Wide Positive Behavioral Interventions and Supports (SWPBIS) have been proposed to address the widespread concern about the high rates of restraint and seclusion. The framework of SWPBIS is an effective and alternative approach to reactive, punitive approaches to problem behaviors in school. According to the National Technical Assistance Center for PBIS, more than 21,600 U.S. schools across all fifty states (representing over 20 percent of schools) were implementing SWPBIS as of 2014.

The SWPBIS is a proactive approach. Its primary goal is to reduce the development of chronic problem behavior and to increase the likelihood of improving academic achievement of all students (Sugai & Horner, 2002). The SWPBIS is consistent with the Response to Intervention model. Its defining feature is the creation of a multitiered system for addressing the needs of all students and preventing school failure (Sugai & Horner, 2009). The most critical aspect of SWPBIS is building a continuum of behavior supports to (a) prevent problems, (b) provide early intervention for students who are at risk of developing repeated challenging behavior, and (c) support students with severe challenging behavior through proactive intensive interventions.

CONTINUUM OF BEHAVIOR SUPPORTS

Building a continuum of behavior supports requires, first, creating a universal behavior support (Tier 1 supports) that can be applied to all students, faculty, staff, and settings within the school. The universal behavior support as the core system creates the foundations of SWPBIS. The foundations involve developing and implementing positively stated school-wide expectations and reinforcement systems Flannery et al. (2013). The identified school-wide expectations are based on current behavior concerns across students and settings (e.g., classrooms, school buses, cafeteria, hallways, and playgrounds). All school personnel are involved in teaching these school-wide expectations to all students across settings.

With universal supports in place, schools have reported significant reductions in bullying (Waasdorp, Bradshaw, & Leaf, 2012), office discipline referrals (Bradshaw, Mitchell, & Leaf, 2010; Nocera, Whitbread, & Nocera, 2014; Sugai et al., 2000; Taylor-Greene et al., 1997), suspensions (Bradshaw et al., 2010; Nocera et al., 2014; Simnsen, 2012), and expulsion (Mathews et al., 2013).

The schools have also reported increases in academic achievement (Bradshaw et al., 2010), social-emotional functioning (Bradshaw, Waasdorp, & Leaf, 2012; McIntosh, 2011), positive student-teacher interactions and teacher self-efficacy (Kelm & MacKintosh, 2012), and positive school climate (Bradshaw, Koth, Thornton, & Leaf, 2009; Nocera et al., 2014).

Although approximately 80 percent of the student body can be successful with universal programs, some students require additional, more intensive behavior supports to be successful in school. Approximately 10 percent–15 percent of the student body will need secondary supports (Tier 2 supports). Tier 2 focuses on explicit instruction of expectations and social skills, and provides a small-group or targeted intervention. Examples of Tier 2 interventions include Check-In/Check-Out (CICO), First Step to Success, mentoring, small-group counseling, social skill instruction, self-management, and group contingencies (Anderson & Borgmeier, 2010).

Tier 2 interventions are designed to be highly efficient and flexible. The interventions are implemented across students exhibiting similar problem behavior and bring about rapid improvement in meeting school-wide expectations (Hawken & Horner, 2003). School social workers, guidance counselors, or behavior specialists typically provide or coordinate Tier 2 interventions. Research indicates that the commonly used Tier 2 interventions are effective across a wide range of acquisition and reduction behaviors of students who are at risk of developing severe challenging behaviors (Ennis, Blair, & George, 2016).

The students who are not responsive to secondary supports (approximately 5 percent of the student body) require a more intensive intervention, referred to as *tertiary support* (Tier 3 supports). Tier 3 supports are designed to address the students' persistent problem behaviors. Such supports promote their school success through a highly individualized PBIS plan. Most of these students will have already been receiving special education services and are frequently removed from the learning environment due to recurrent or significantly dangerous or disruptive behaviors.

In addition to the individualized PBIS plan, wraparound mental health services are typically implemented to support this small number of students (Scott & Eber, 2003). A handful of studies have reported positive outcomes for behavior, social-emotional, and academic performance of the Tier 3 supports across various students with severe problem behavior (Iovannone et al., 2009; Lane, Kalberg, & Shepcaro, 2009; Loman & Horner, 2012). It is recommended that interventions for these students should be linked to the SWPBIS system to achieve maximum outcomes (Newcomer & Powers, 2002).

CORE COMPONENTS OF AND CONTRIBUTING FACTORS FOR SUCCESSFUL SWPBIS

To implement effectively the continuum of support and to prevent problems, schools must optimize the core components (foundational systems) of SWPBIS. The core components include (a) identification of school-wide academic and behavioral outcomes, (b) establishment of organizational systems, (c) implementation of evidence-based practices, and (d) use of data to guide decision-making (Sugai & Horner, 2006).

School-wide outcomes require clear definitions of school-wide expectations and a focus on instruction and reinforcement of the school-wide expectations during SWPBIS implementation. The establishment of organizational systems (e.g., supports, resources, training) is essential to support and sustain implementation of SWPBIS and achieve specific academic and behavioral outcomes. SWPBIS stresses the use of evidence-based practices in supporting students at each tier. SWPBIS also emphasizes the use of data to make decisions about the selection, implementation, and progress-monitoring of interventions.

Use of data involves monitoring intervention implementation and student response to intervention by analyzing a variety of data (Sugai et al., 2010). Data include implementation fidelity, systems-level implementation evaluation, office discipline referral, suspension, detention, and attendance, and other indirect and direct observational data on problem behavior (Sugai et al.,

2010). These data help determine whether the interventions were implemented as planned and students are responding to the interventions or require additional supports (Sugai et al., 2010).

FACTORS CONTRIBUTING TO SUCCESSFUL IMPLEMENTATION AND SUSTAINABILITY OF SWPBIS

Although positive student outcomes of SWPBIS have been documented, continuation of the outcomes depends on the sustainability of SWPBIS implementation (Fixsen, Naoom, Blasé, Fiedman, & Wallace, 2005). The key factors that contribute to successful implementation and sustainability of SWPBIS have been found to be the following: (a) a team-based approach at all levels, (b) data-based decision-making, and (c) building the intervention infrastructure (Benazzi, Horner, & Good, 2006; Colvin, 2007; Sugai et al., 2010). Student and staff buy-in, administrator support, establishment of system-level data, and alignment of SWPBIS with other school initiatives have also been found to be key factors associated with the success of SWPBIS (Flannery, Fenning, Kato, & McIntosh, 2014). Additional factors include engaging students, staff, and families and ongoing training of staff during the process of implementing the SWPBIS across all tiers (Sugai et al., 2010).

DIGITAL AND ONLINE LEARNING FOR STUDENTS WITH DISABILITIES

Along with SWPBIS, school leaders should envision themselves providing online education for K–12 students with disabilities. The Internet became mainstream in most U.S. households in early 2000s (Greenstein, 2015). This trend has made the face of education rapidly change from traditional brick-and-mortar classroom settings to online and virtual platforms. Online learning environments have tremendously grown and expanded higher education opportunities for many learners, particularly those in remote areas with limited access to traditional classroom instruction (Dell, Dell, & Blackwell, 2015).

Trends in K–12 education appear to be following the same path, with many states reporting increases in online programs, with estimates of several million students participating nationwide (Burdette, Greer, & Woods, 2013; Picciano & Seaman, 2009; Watson, Murin, Vashaw, Gemin, & Rapp, 2013). While benefits to this transition exist for many students, online learning environments pose challenges for student with disabilities.

This group makes up approximately 13 percent of the K–12 student population, roughly 6.5 million students in total (National Center for Education

Statistics, 2016). Among the barriers students with disabilities face are inadequate preparation, insufficient support, and limited communication (Burdette et al., 2013; National Association of State Directors of Special Education, 2009).

PREPARATION OF ONLINE LEARNING ENVIRONMENTS

Preparing online programs for students with disabilities requires assurance that the program is accessible to all students, that accommodations and related services are provided, and that IEPs are being developed and implemented. This online learning has proven to be particularly difficult for students with moderate to severe disabilities as many online learning environments are unable to adequately accommodate them (Burdette et al., 2013; Shah, 2011).

While data are limited on accessibility of K–12 online programs for students with disabilities, evidence shows that accessibility standards are not being met. Basham, Stahl, Ortiz, Rice, and Smith (2015) reported that only 36 percent of online learning programs in the nation pledge to be accessible for students with disabilities.

Of these programs, only 2 percent of them had established systems for data collection and monitoring of students with disabilities (Basham et al., 2015). The recently released annual report of the Center on Online Learning and Students with Disabilities (COLSD) (2016) revealed that approximately 75 percent of states provided unclear information or no mention of the IDEA in their policy documents pertaining to online learning environments.

In light of this information, it is imperative that visionary school leaders and educators are well versed in, and actively recognize, the guidelines set forth in IDEA still readily apply, and must be followed for students with disabilities to ensure that they are receiving a FAPE in the least restrictive environment. To serve students appropriately with disabilities, online learning environments need to provide full access to the curriculum, which includes providing individualized instruction and adequate accommodations to each student for all materials, assignments, and discussions.

Additionally, IEPs including all accommodations and related services must be incorporated into online learning environments for students with disabilities, although currently no guidelines are set forth for how this is to be accomplished. However, two standards have been created to assist designers of online learning environments in verifying whether their programs are adequately accessible: the Web Content Accessibility Guideline (WCAG) 2.0 (World Wide Web Consortium, 2011) and the amended Section 508 of the Workforce Rehabilitation Act of 1973 (2000). The accessibility of information covered under these standards generally applies only to individuals with sensory and physical disabilities, while not taking into account students with other disabilities (Smith & Harvey, 2014).

As such, the content presented in both elementary and secondary online programs was not designed to meet the needs of students with disabilities (COLSD, 2016). One reason is that accessible instructional materials used in traditional schools are typically *print* materials that cannot easily be adapted for use in online learning environments. Furthermore, resources are not specifically investigated for accessibility, although the ability for educators to recognize and select accessible materials is vital (Hashey & Stahl, 2014).

Technology in general focuses on what students with disabilities "can" do, rather than can't do. Students in online learning environments—particularly those in asynchronous course settings—have limited direct contact and communication with their teachers in real time. Given that students with disabilities often require more individualized attention and support—as well as more frequent and explicit communication with teachers—this puts them at a disadvantage in online learning environments (Basham et al., 2015; Greer, Rowland, & Smith, 2014).

Additionally, such environments vary greatly in regard to requirements for frequency of check-ins with students, monitoring, and availability of support staff. Rice and Carter (2015a) reported that K–12 grade teachers found it difficult to fully support their students because of a lack of support they themselves are experiencing. With severely lacking laws and policies in online learning, teachers in these settings require different skill sets to address the instructional, legal, and ethical implications of educating individuals with disabilities (Basham et al., 2015; Rice & Carter, 2015b).

In online learning environments, teachers have limited opportunity to observe, challenge, motivate, and provide corrective feedback to students (Wright, 2007). Thus, teachers require effective communication skills in various platforms such as phone calls, e-mail, video conferences, online chats, and written instructions to interact effectively with students and parents alike. Contacting each individual student—or parent—requires much additional instructional time in not only content areas but also in how to access course content by tapping into additional resources (Rice & Carter, 2015b).

Communication and support are less prevalent not only between students and staff but also among students. Many students with disabilities, particularly those with social and communication disorders, are already at a disadvantage socially. With the push toward online learning where interactions are limited to use in expanding learning, it is feared that these individuals will fall further behind socially and emotionally (Florida Virtual School, 2012).

To address this issue, Murphy (2004) proposed a model of collaboration that encourages students to interact with one another in ways that are more meaningful where they work together toward a shared goal. While other similar recommendations of incorporating social and collaborative practices in online learning exist (e.g., Roblyer & Wiencke, 2003; Smith et al., 2015), no standard guidelines or oversight are offered.

No doubt that educating students online is time-consuming for parents and requires increased involvement across many domains such as student motivation, instruction, addressing behavior, and administrative tasks (Ahn, 2011; Huerta & Gonzalez, 2004; Bogden, 2003; McCluskey, 2002). Parents of students with disabilities have even greater responsibility to assist their children in additional areas of organization of materials and time, comprehension and completion of assignments, learning and understanding of course content, and skills that address social and behavioral issues (Burdette & Greer, 2014).

Especially in situations where no special education teacher is assigned, parents are expected to take on a role similar to that of the educator and must be readily available for instruction. A study found that 50 percent of parents of K–8 students committed more than three hours per day to their child's schooling (Burdette & Greer, 2014).

WAYS THAT VISIONARY SCHOOL LEADERS GUIDE TEACHERS IN PREPARING STUDENTS

The rapidly changing nature of education poses an equal number of challenges for school leaders and administrators when overseeing and implementing online learning programs for students with disabilities. According to Carter and Rice (2016), school administrators are only beginning to understand what needs to be done to improve teachers' knowledge of technology and how to use these resources to enhance student learning.

Fortunately, resources and standards are being developed and adjusted to give guidance and address issues as they arise in online learning. School leaders can assist teachers in making informed educational decisions for students with disabilities. The leaders will be able to assist by staying abreast of current research and resources available themselves.

The International Association of K–12 Online Learning (2011) developed the National Standards for Quality Online Teaching Version 2 (iNACOL V2) to delineate expectations set forth for online educators (table 4.1). The standards align with those of the CEC and are therefore relevant to students with disabilities. The iNACOL V2 not only outlines what online educators should know but also includes how they should perform by offering rubrics (see Cooper & Gargan, 2009) and scoring guides under each standard.

It is crucial to provide tools to assist teachers in selecting materials and resources that improve accessibility to students with disabilities (Hashey & Stahl, 2014). The Voluntary Product Accessibility Template (VPAT) as

Table 4.1. National Standards for Quality Online Teaching Version 2 (iNACOL V2; International Association of K–12 Online Learning, 2011)

Standard A	The online teacher knows the primary concepts and structures of effective online instruction and is able to create learning experiences to enable student success.
Standard B	The online teacher understands and is able to use a range of technologies, both existing and emerging, that effectively support student learning and engagement in the online environment.
Standard C	The online teacher plans, designs, and incorporates strategies to encourage active learning, application, interaction, participation, and collaboration in the online environment.
Standard D	The online teacher promotes student success through clear expectations, prompt responses, and regular feedback.
Standard E	The online teacher models, guides, and encourages legal, ethical, and safe behavior related to technology use.
Standard F	The online teacher is cognizant of the diversity of student academic needs and incorporates accommodations into the online environment.
Standard G	The online teacher demonstrates competencies in creating and implementing assessments in online learning environments in ways that ensure validity and reliability of the instruments and procedures.
Standard H	The online teacher develops and delivers assessments, projects, and assignments that meet standards-based learning goals and assesses learning progress by measuring student achievement of the learning goals.
Standard I	The online teacher demonstrates competency in using data from assessments and other data sources to modify content and to guide student learning.
Standard J	The online teacher interacts in a professional, effective manner with colleagues, parents, and other members of the community to support students' success.
Standard K	The online teacher arranges media and content to help students and teachers transfer knowledge most effectively in the online environment.

outlined under Section 508 is just such a resource and was generated as a guide for educators, which provides accessibility information for products and materials. Schools should use this document to promote products that meet the standards set forth in Section 508. The VPAT often works in combination with the Government Product Accessibility Template that has set accessibility requirements for products and services.

While resources such as the VPAT provide educators with information on accessible tools for students, Universal Design for Learning (UDL) offers a framework for instructional planning and practice in online learning. Three overarching principles in UDL include the following: (1) provide multiple means of representation, the "what" of learning; (2) use multiple means of action and expression, the "how" on learning; and (3) have multiple means of engagement, the "why" of learning National Center on Universal Design for Learning at Center for Applied Special Technology [CAST], (2012). These principles are further broken down into the following standards (see table 4.1):

The incorporation of UDL provides benefits to all students by allowing easier access and navigation of all course materials.

Virtual learning platforms can easily incorporate numerous combinations of audio, video, text, and many other methods to present and communicate information. This offers the opportunity for all students to have improved access to curricula when given numerous outlets for expression and participation (Hashey & Stahl, 2014). In alignment with UDL, online instruction could open up a world of possibilities to students by offering content presented in multiple, accessible ways to enhance comprehension, learning, and overall academic achievement.

CONCLUSION

The active visionary role of school leaders is critical for increased educational outcomes for students with disabilities in inclusive and other educational settings. School leaders can achieve this goal by offering well-rounded education and creating safe and healthy school environments. To assist students with disabilities in transitioning from traditional classrooms to online and virtual classrooms, school leaders must be familiar with, and integrate, technology into education effectively. We proposed the three features that school leaders envision themselves being familiar with, planning, and implementing in the near future.

Federal education laws provide rights and protections to students with disabilities and their parents. These laws have been frequently updated and reauthorized. The ESSA (2015), the new name of the *No Child Left Behind* (NCLB), was recently signed into the law. In late 2016, Congress began to prepare reauthorization of the IDEA (2004). As having profoundly affected the education of students with disabilities, visionary school leaders must be—and stay—abreast with the changes and updates and plan to implement the reauthorized laws.

For SWPBIS to be successfully implemented, school leaders should possess the following leadership practices or dimensions: (1) establishing goals and expectations; (2) practicing strategic resourcing; (3) planning, coordinating, and evaluating teaching and the curriculum; (4) promoting and participating in teacher learning and development; and (5) ensuring an orderly and supportive environment (Robinson, Lloyd, & Rowe, 2008). Of these leadership dimensions, *promoting and participating in teacher learning and development* enables teachers to make and sustain changes in practices, and has been found to be most strongly associated with positive student outcomes (Robinson et al., 2008).

School leaders should provide continued professional development and support to staff during implementation of the SWPBIS, given that staff training and ongoing professional development are one of the key factors for sustainable implementation of SWPBIS (Bradshaw & Pas, 2011; McIntosh et al., 2013). However, capacity building of the school-based team—through ongoing coaching and technical assistance by a district leadership team—is crucial to enhance sustainability (Mcintosh et al., 2013; Santangelo, 2009). A reduction in district technical assistance leads to practice abandonment (Santangelo, 2009). We urge visionary leaders to join in other schools that have successfully implemented SWPBIS.

Students in grades K–12 will likely interact with their teachers and peers remotely. To do so, they need to be comfortable with and able to use technology. Joe Williams, executive director of Democrats for Education Reform, says: "With some exciting exceptions, public schools are one of the few institutions in modern life that have not seen radical changes spurred by technology." Jake Schwartz, CEO and cofounder of General Assembly, predicts that as technology advances, its limits will become clear. Nevertheless, when visionary leaders strategically plan and implement what is necessary for their school, they will accomplish the goal of student success.

REFERENCES

Ahn, J. (2011). The effect of social network sites on adolescents' social and academic development: Current theories and controversies. *Journal of the American Society for Information Science and Technology*, 62(8), 1435–1445.

Alvarez, B. (2016, June 30). Promising changes for special education under ESSA. *News and Features from the National Education Association*. Retrieved from http://neatoday.org/2016/06/30/special-education-essa/

Anderson, C. M., & Borgmeier, C. (2010). Tier II interventions within the framework of school-wide positive behavior support: Essential features for design, implementation, and maintenance. *Behavior Analysis in Practice*, 3, 33–45.

Basham, J. D., Stahl, S., Ortiz, K., Rice, M. F., Smith, S. (2015). *Equity matters: Digital & online learning for students with disabilities*. Lawrence, KS: Center on Online Learning and Students with Disabilities.

Benazzi, L., Horner, R. H., & Good, R. H. (2006). Effects of behavior support team composition on the technical adequacy and contextual fit of behavior support plans. *The Journal of Special Education*, 40, 160–170.

Bogden, J. (2003). Cyber charter schools: A new breed in the education corral. *The State Education Standard*, 4(3), 33–37.

Bradshaw, C. P., Koth, C. W., Thornton, L. A., & Leaf, P. J. (2009). Altering school climate through school-wide Positive Behavioral Interventions and Supports: Findings from a group-randomized effectiveness trial. *Prevention science*, *10*, 100–115.

Bradshaw, C. P., Mitchell, M. M., & Leaf, P. J. (2010). Examining the effects of school wide positive behavioral interventions and supports on student outcomes results from a randomized controlled effectiveness trial in elementary schools. *Journal of Positive Behavior Interventions*, *12*, 133–148.

Bradshaw, C. P., & Pas, E. T. (2011). A statewide scale up of positive behavioral interventions and supports: A description of the development of systems of support and analysis of adoption and implementation. *School Psychology Review*, *40*, 530.

Bradshaw, C. P., Waasdorp, T. E., & Leaf, P. J. (2012). Effects of school-wide positive behavioral interventions and supports on child behavior problems. *Pediatrics*, *130*, e1136–e1145.

Burdette, P. (2010). *Principal preparedness to support students with disabilities and other diverse learners*. Alexandria, VA: National Association of State Directors of Special Education.

Burdette, P. J., & Greer, D. L. (2014). Online Learning and Students with Disabilities: Parent Perspectives. *Journal of Interactive Online Learning*, *13*(2), 67–88.

Burdette, P. J., Greer, D. L., & Woods, K. L. (2013). K–12 online learning and students with disabilities: Perspectives from state special education directors. *Journal of Asynchronous Learning Networks*, *17*, 65–72.

Carter, R. A., & Rice, M. F. (2016). Administrator work in leveraging technologies for students with disabilities in online coursework. *Journal of Special Education Technology*, *31*, 137–146.

CAST (2012). *Universal Design for Learning*. Retrieved from http://www.cast.org/our-work/about-udl.html#.WH1KI7YrK8V

Center on Online Learning and Students with Disabilities (2016). Equity Matters 2016: Digital and Online Learning for Students with Disabilities. Retrieved from http://centerononlinelearning.org/

Cole, S. (2015, March 10). 5 big ways education will change by 2020. *Fast Company Leadership*. Retrieved from https://www.fastcompany.com/3043387/sector-forecasting/5-big-ways-education-will-change-by-2020

Colvin, G. (2007). *Seven steps for developing a proactive school wide discipline plan: A guide for principals and leadership teams*. Thousand Oaks, CA: Corwin Press.

Cooper, B. S., & Gargan, A. (2009). Rubrics in education: Old term, new meanings. *Phi Delta Kappan* (May/June/July 2009), 54–55.

Council for Exceptional Children. (n.d.). *CEC opposes new IDEA regulations on selected issues*. Arlington, VA: Council for Exceptional Children. Retrieved from http://www.cec.sped.org/Policy-and-Advocacy/Current-Sped-Gifted-Issues/Individuals-with-Disabilities-Education-Act/CEC-Opposes-New-IDEA-Regulations-on-Selected-Issues

Council for Exceptional Children. (n.d.). *Special Educator Professional Preparation: Special Educator Preparation Standards*. Retrieved from https://www.cec.sped.org/Standards/Special-Educator-Professional-Preparation-Standards

Dell, C. A., Dell, T. F., & Blackwell, T. L. (2015). Applying universal design for learning in online courses: Pedagogical and practical considerations. *Journal of Educators Online*, *12*, 166–192.

Ennis, C., Blair, K. C., & George, H. P. (2016). An evaluation of group contingency interventions: The role of teacher preference. *Journal of Positive Behavior Interventions, 18,* 17–28.

Fabelo, T., et al. or Thompson, M. D., Plotkin, M., Carmichael, D., Marchbanks, M. P., & Booth, E. A. (2011). *Breaking schools' rules: A statewide study of how school discipline relates to students' success and juvenile justice involvement.* New York: Council of State Governments Justice Center. Retrieved from justicecenter.csg.org/resources/juveniles.

Feng, L., & Sass, T. (2012). *Competing risks analysis of dropout and educational attainment of students with disabilities* (Working Paper 12–09). Atlanta, GA: Andrew Young School of Policy Studies.

Fixsen, D. L., Naoom, S. F., Blase, K. A., Friedman, R. M., & Wallace, F. (2005). *Implementation Research: A Synthesis of the Literature.*

Flannery, K. B., Fenning, P., Kato, M. M., & McIntosh, K. (2014). Effects of school-wide positive behavioral interventions and supports and fidelity of implementation on problem behavior in high schools. *School Psychology Quarterly, 29*(2), 111–125.

Flannery, K. B., Frank, J. L., Kato, M. M., Doren, B., & Fenning, P. (2013). Implementing school wide positive behavior support in high school settings: Analysis of eight high schools. *The High School Journal, 96,* 267–282.

Florida Virtual School. (2012). Exceptional student education. Retrieved from https://www.flvs.net/about/programs/exceptional-student-education

Gershoff, E.T., & Font, S. A. (2016). Corporal Punishment in U.S. Public Schools: Prevalence, Disparities in Use, and Status in State and Federal Policy. *Society for Research in Child Development 30*(1), pp. 1–7.

Greenstein, S. (2015). *How the Internet became commercial.* Princeton, NJ: Princeton University Press. Retrieved from http://press.princeton.edu/titles/10574.html

Greer, D., Rowland, A., & Smith, S. (2014). Critical considerations for teaching students with disabilities in online environments. *TEACHING Exceptional Children, 46*(5), 79–91.

Hashey, A., & Stahl, S. (2014). Making online learning accessible for students with disabilities. *TEACHING Exceptional Children, 46*(5), 70–78.

Hawken, L. S., & Horner, R. H. (2003). Evaluation of a targeted intervention within a school wide system of behavior support. *Journal of Behavioral Education, 12,* 225–240.

Huerta, L., & Gonzalez, M. (2004). Cyber and home charter schools: How states are defining new forms of public schooling. Unpublished manuscript, Teachers College-Columbia University/University of California at Berkley.

International Association of K–12 Online Learning (2011). National Standards for Quality Online Teaching Version 2. Retrieved from http://www.inacol.org/resource/inacol-national-standards-for-quality-online-teaching-v2/

Iovannone, R., Greenbaum, P. E., Wang, W., Kincaid, D., Dunlap, G., & Strain, P. (2009). Randomized controlled trial of the prevent-teach-reinforce (PTR) tertiary intervention for students with problem behaviors. *Journal of Emotional and Behavioral Disorders, 17,* 213–225.

Kelm, J. L., & McIntosh, K. (2012). Effects of school-wide positive behavior support on teacher self-efficacy. *Psychology in the Schools, 49,* 137–147.

Lane, K. L., Kalberg, J. R., & Shepcaro, J. C. (2009). An examination of the evidence base for function-based interventions for students with emotional and/or behavioral disorders attending middle and high schools. *Council for Exceptional Children, 75*, 321–340.

Lewis, T. J., Powers, L. J., Kely, M. J., & Newcomer, L. L. (2002). Reducing problem behaviors on the playground: An investigation of the application of school wide positive behavior supports. *Psychology in the Schools, 39*, 181–190.

Loman, S., & Horner, R. H. (2013). Examining the efficacy of a basic functional behavioral assessment training package for school personnel. *Journal of Positive Behavior Interventions, 16*, 18–30.

Lopes, J. A., Monteiro, I., & Sil, V. (2004). Teachers' perceptions about teaching problem students in regular classrooms. *Education and Treatment of Children, 27*(4), 394–419.

Mathews, S., McIntosh, K., Frank, J. L., & May, S. L. (2013). Critical features predicting sustained implementation of school-wide positive behavioral interventions and supports. *Journal of Positive Behavior Interventions, 16*, 168–178.

McCann, C. (2014). *Federal funding for students with disabilities: The evolution of federal special education finance in the United States*. Washington, DC: New America Education Policy Program. Retrieved from https://na-production.s3.amazonaws.com/documents/federal-funding-for-students-with-disabilities.pdf

McCluskey, N. (2002). Beyond brick and mortar: Cyber charters revolutionizing education (CER action paper). Retrieved from http://virtualschooling.wordpress.com/2005/11/23/beyond-brick-and-mortar-cyber-charters-revolutionizing-education-cer-action-paper/

McIntosh, K., Bennett, J. L., & Price, K. (2011). Evaluation of social and academic effects of school-wide positive behaviour support in a Canadian school district. *Exceptionality Education International, 21*, 46–60.

McIntosh, K., Mercer, S. H., Hume, A. E., Frank, J. L., Turri, M. G., & Mathews, S. (2013). Factors related to sustained implementation of school wide positive behavior support. *Exceptional Children, 79*, 293.

Michigan School Business Officials. (2016, June). U.S. Department of Education provides updated FAQs for ESSA. eNews & Views. Retrieved from http://www.msbo.org/newsletter/us-department-education-provides-updated-faqs-essa

Murphy, E. (2004). Recognizing and promoting collaboration in an online asynchronous discussion. *British Journal of Educational Technology, 35*(4), 421–431.

National Association of State Directors of Special Education. (2009). National Implementation of Response to Intervention (RTI): Research Summary. Retrieved from http://www.nasdse.org/Portals/0/NationalImplementationofRTI-Research-Summary.pdf

National Center for Education Statistics. (2016). Digest of Education Statistics 50th Edition. Retrieved from https://nces.ed.gov/pubs2016/2016006.pdf

Nocera, E. J., Whitbread, K. M., & Nocera, G. P. (2014). Impact of school-wide positive behavior supports on student behavior in the middle grades. *Research in Middle Level Education Online, 37*, 1–14.

Office of Special Education and Rehabilitative Services. (2014). *36th annual report to Congress on the implementation of the Individuals with Disabilities Education Act, 2014*. Washington, DC: U.S. Department of Education.

Pacer Center. (2010). Pacer Center action information sheets: Changes in IDEA involve parents' rights. Retrieved from http://www.pacer.org/parent/php/PHP-c173.pdf

Picciano, A. G., & Seaman, J. (2009). K–12 Online Learning: A 2008 Follow-Up of the Survey of U.S. School District Administrators. Retrieved from http://files.eric.ed.gov/fulltext/ED530104.pdf

PSEA Education Services Division. (2016). The Every Student Succeeds Act: Special education requirements. Retrieved from https://www.psea.org/uploadedFiles/Publications/Professional_Publications/Advisories/Advisory-ESSA-SpecialEducation.pdf

Rice, M., & Carter, R. A. (2015a). When we talk about compliance it's because we lived it: Online educators' experiences supporting students with disabilities. *Online Learning Journal, 19*, 18–36.

Rice, M., & Carter, R. A. (2015b). With new eyes: Online teachers' sacred stories of students with disabilities. In Rice M. (Ed.) *Exploring pedagogies for diverse learners online* (pp. 205–226). Bingley, UK: Emerald Group Publishing.

Robinson, V. M., Lloyd, C. A., & Rowe, K. J. (2008). The impact of leadership on student outcomes: An analysis of the differential effects of leadership types. *Educational Administration Quarterly, 44*, 635–674.

Roblyer, M. D., & Wiencke, W. R. (2003). Design and use of a rubric to assess and encourage interactive qualities in distance courses. *The American Journal of Distance Education, 17*(2), 77–98.

Santangelo, T. (2009). Collaborative problem solving effectively implemented, but not sustained: A case for aligning the sun, the moon, and the stars. *Exceptional Children, 75*, 185–209.

Santoli, S. P., Sachs, J., Romey, E. A., & McClurg, S. (2008). A successful formula for middle-school inclusion: Collaboration, time, and administrative support. *Research in Middle Level Education Online, 32*(2), 1–13.

Scott, T. M., & Eber, L. (2003). Functional assessment and wraparound as systemic school processes: primary, secondary, and tertiary systems examples. *Journal of Positive Behavior Interventions, 5*, 131–143.

Shah, N. (2011). eLearning access for special-needs students. *Education Week, 31*(1), S2–S4.

Smith, S. J., & Harvey, E. E. (2014). K–12 online lesson alignment to the principles of Universal Design for Learning: The Khan Academy. *Open Learning: The Journal of Open, Distance and e-Learning, 29*(3), 222–242.

Sugai, G., & Horner, R. (2002). The evolution of discipline practices: School-wide positive behavior supports. *Child & Family Behavior Therapy, 24*, 23–50.

Sugai, G., & Horner, R. H. (2009). Responsiveness-to-intervention and school-wide positive behavior supports: Integration of multi-tiered system approaches. *Exceptionality, 17*, 223–237.

Sugai, G., Horner, R. H., Algozzine, R., Barrett, S., Lewis, T., Anderson, C., & Simonsen, B. (2010). School-wide positive behavior support: Implementers' blueprint and self-assessment. Eugene, OR: University of Oregon.

Sugai, G., Horner, R. H., Dunlap, G., Hieneman, M., Lewis, T. J., Nelson, C. M., . . . & Turnbull, H. R. (2000). Applying positive behavior support and functional behavioral assessment in schools. *Journal of Positive Behavior Interventions, 2*, 131–143.

Sugai, G., & Horner, R. R. (2006). A promising approach for expanding and sustaining school-wide positive behavior support. *School Psychology Review, 35*, 245.

Taylor-Greene, S., Brown, D., Nelson, L., Longton, J., Gassman, T., Cohen, J., . . . & Hall, S. (1997). School-wide behavioral support: Starting the year off right. *Journal of Behavioral Education, 7*, 99–112.

U.S. Department of Education. (2006). Analysis of comments and changes. *Federal Register, 71*(156), 46540–46752. Retrieved from http://www.parentcenterhub.org/wp-content/uploads/repo_items/IDEA2004regulations.pdf

U.S. Department of Education. (2008). Assistance to states for the education of children with disabilities and preschool grants for children with disabilities; Final rule. *Federal Register, 73*(231), 73005–73029. Retrieved from https://www2.ed.gov/legislation/FedRegister/finrule/2008-4/120108a.pdf

U.S. Department of Education. (2016). Every Student Succeeds Act (ESSA). Retrieved from http://www.ed.gov/essa

U.S. Department of State Information Resource Management Impact Program for Accessible Computer/Communication Technology. (2015). Government Product Accessibility Template. Retrieved from https://www.state.gov/documents/organization/198867.pdf

U.S. Department of State Information Resource Management Impact Program for Accessible Computer/Communication Technology. (2015). Voluntary Product Accessibility Template. Retrieved from https://www.state.gov/documents/organization/126552.pdf

Waasdorp, T. E., Bradshaw, C. P., & Leaf, P. J. (2012). The impact of school-wide positive behavioral interventions and supports on bullying and peer rejection: A randomized controlled effectiveness trial. *Archives of Pediatrics & Adolescent Medicine, 166*, 149–156.

Watson, J., Murin, A., Vashaw, L., Gemin, B., & Rapp, C. (2013). Keeping pace with K–12 online & blended learning: An annual review of policy and practice. Durango, CO: Evergreen Education Group.

Workforce Rehabilitation Act of 1973. (2000). Section 508 Standards for Electronic and Information Technology. Retrieved from https://www.access-board.gov/guidelines-and-standards/communications-and-it/about-the-section-508-standards/section-508-standards

World Wide Web Consortium. (2011). *Web Contact Accessibility Guidelines 2.0*. Retrieved from https://www.w3.org/WAI/WCAG20/glance/

Wright, C. R. (2007). Adapting learning materials for distance learning. *Knowledge series: A topical, start-up guide to distance education practice and delivery*. Vancouver, BC: Commonwealth of Learning.

Wright, P. (2016). *IDEA reauthorization: Sample letter with background info & references*. Retrieved from http://www.wrightslaw.com/news/04/idea.reauth.1109.ltr.htm

Wrightslaw, P. (2016). *IDEA reauthorization: Sample letter with background info & references*. Retrieved from http://www.wrightslaw.com/news/04/idea.reauth.1109.ltr.htm

Chapter 5

Improving Student Outcomes through Reflective Practice and Mindfulness in Educational Leadership

Lisa Bass

School leadership is critical to reaching student achievement and success. According to Bush (2009), a growing recognition around the world appears in both developed and developing countries that schools require effective leaders if they are to provide the best possible learning environment for their students. Leithwood, Day, Sammons, Harris, and Hopkins (2006) further note that school principals are second only to classroom teaching as an influence on student achievement.

Principals are responsible for both the teachers in their building and the actual teaching that occurs in each classroom—as these leaders are charged with managing and maintaining human resources as well as instructional leadership. The job of the school principal is ever-expanding and is growing more demanding as their responsibilities and accountability increase (Walker & Qian, 2006).

The work of an educational leader is filled with challenges, variability, and constant change. Most school leaders can attest to that no two days are exactly the same. One of the most challenging qualities of the work of educational leaders is that they must be able to deal with multiple issues and constituents, and on many different levels. School leaders manage issues that include the maintenance of, or emergencies in, the physical plant; human resource issues, from teacher shortage to the effectiveness of faculty and staff; serving the parents; and instituting instructional leadership that produces student achievement. Educational leaders experience a variety of challenges that require them to employ strategies to help them manage their school while maintaining their personal lives and their sanity.

To accomplish these goals, they must build upon their experiences meaningfully to run their schools in ways that most benefit students and support the successful management of the school. In order to build upon their experiences meaningfully, two philosophical practices can be employed, which on the surface appear to be diametrically opposed, however work together. These practices, reflective practice and mindfulness, will be discussed in this chapter.

REFLECTIVE PRACTICES

Reflection, though often neglected, is a natural, essential, and important tool to be used in management (Hedberg, 2009). John Dewey (1933, p. 9) is credited with bringing the notion of reflection to education, and defines reflection as "active persistent and careful consideration of any belief or supposed form of knowledge." Reflection and vision are key concepts in leadership that guide leaders in improving their practice. Hedberg (2009, p. 12) explains reflection as "a cognitive function that involves consideration, contemplation, speculation, musing, and pondering."

As Keogh and Walker (1985c) further note that reflection/vision is the "activity in which people recapture their experience, think about it, mull it over, and evaluate it" (p. 33). In this recapturing, thinking, and mulling, leaders have an opportunity to consider their actions and the resulting consequences. Thoughtful leaders may even take the time to consider alternative actions and possible outcomes. Osterman and Kottkamp (1993) connect reflective practice to professional growth and development, noting that as practitioners gain self-awareness about the impact of their performance, such awareness creates opportunity for growth and development.

This connection between practice and professional growth is demonstrative of the origin of reflective practice being experiential learning. According to this theory, professional learning does not take place until the practitioner is on the job. Osterman and Kottkamp (1993) further provide the metaphor of the reflective practitioners as visionary actors and critics.

As an actor, the reflective practitioner recalls and recognizes his or her visions and actions; as a critic, he or she considers the impact of his or her performance. Reflection facilitates the most thoughtful and wise decision-making possible. Without such reflection and vision, leaders may make rash decisions that they may come to regret—and might not learn from their errors, which limits their ability to improve their vision and decision-making. According to Jordi (2011), "reflection is predominantly conceptualized as the rational analytical process through which human beings extract knowledge from their experience" (p. 181).

Effective leaders are known to revisit and revise their practice continuously to improve it. Over time, such improvements serve to mark their growth as a leader. Schon (1983) grounds professional knowledge in professional experience. In other words, practitioners learn from their professional experiences as they make sense of them. Without the agency of reflection, most practitioners are unable to articulate their knowledge as they exhibit vision, tacit knowledge, or knowing-in-practice.

Consequently, leaders are not able to reveal what or how they are being effective (Osterman & Kottkamp, 1993). To move to a place where leaders can benefit from their tacit knowledge to the point where they can articulate their knowledge into a working theory of action, they must engage in reflective practice to the point where their vision and knowledge are explicit. Explicit knowledge and a clear vision lead to consistent management practice.

Osterman and Kottkamp (1993) provide an example of how reflective practice and vision were used in a school district to improve practice by an administrative group when the superintendent was not pleased with student's reactions to their exchange experience in Moscow. The superintendent felt that the students did not adequately reflect their experiences, and that they lacked feeling. In his words, "they followed the essay form but communicated little meaning." As the group analyzed the problem, a broader concern emerged from their discussions.

The focus moved from the quality of student essays to the reality that the instructional orientation did not foster the learning outcomes that educators envisioned. The new problem statement became: "How do we as district leaders work to transform an instructional orientation we believe does not result in the best possible education?" (Osterman & Kottkamp, 1993, p. 7). This new orientation led to a new ongoing focus for group reflection for these leaders.

Vince and Reynolds (2004) argue that reflection is imperative to the lives of managers as it becomes part of what it means to lead and manage. In fact, they believe that reflection should be included in the day-to-day lives of managers—rather than a disconnected, separate activity; and that it should be central and supported by structures and the culture of the workplace. They further postulate that reflection and vision should affect decisions and choices, policies and activities, and the politics and emotions associated with them.

Reflective practice is especially essential to successful school leadership due to the fluid nature of the business of school. In addition to the long list of variable factors noted earlier, fluidity can be further marked by the rapid changes in school district policy and ever-changing budgetary concerns. School leaders and policy makers must consider multiple moving parts in their decision-making. Careful consideration includes the mulling over of decisions in leadership practice as discussed earlier. The mulling over that occurs in the moment of decision-making can be described as mindfulness.

MINDFULNESS DEFINED

The word *mindful* is often used when describing the importance and vision of paying attention to details, or the state of being alert. However, *mindfulness* takes the meaning of being mindful a step further. Mindfulness can be described as the state of being steeped in the present moment—while other thoughts are blocked out. Mindfulness can also be characterized by careful observations, being compassionate, nonjudgmental, and exercising restraint when prudent before reacting.

To engage in mindfulness is to be completely aware of one's surroundings and to hone in on the ability to focus on one thing at a time. Langer (1989) described mindfulness as a creative cognitive process. According to Kabat-Zinn (1990), mindfulness is a process of bringing a certain quality of attention to moment-by-moment experience. However, in the purest and simplest form, mindfulness is the act of being fully aware while living in, and fully appreciating, the present moment without judgment when considering the environment around oneself (Germer, 2004).

Bishop et al. (2004) note that "mindfulness in contemporary psychology has been adopted as an approach for increasing awareness and responding skillfully to mental processes that contribute to emotional distress and maladaptive behavior" (p. 230). Noticing a gap in the literature, Bishop et al. (2004) set out to form a more complete definition for mindfulness, and proposed one with two components. The first part of mindfulness, as defined by Bishop et al. (2004), is self-regulation of attention.

Mindful practitioners learn to become more aware of the current experiences by observing and giving attention to the changing field of thoughts, feelings, and sensations from moment to moment and regulating the focus of their attention. This focused attention leads to a feeling of alertness to the here and now, described as being fully present, alive, and in the moment. Researchers have found that the development of mindfulness in individuals would lead to improvements in sustained attention (Klee & Garfinkel, 1983; Rogers & Monsell, 1995) and in cognitive inhibition (Bishop et al., 2004).

In addition to the self-regulation of attention, Bishop et al. (2004) indicated that mindfulness is "further defined by an orientation to an experience that is adopted and cultivated in mindfulness meditation practices" (p. 233). As such, practitioners of mindfulness are instructed to take note of their thoughts, feelings, and experiences. With all thoughts believed to be worthy of initial exploration, mindfulness has been conceptualized as a process of relating openly with experience, similar to experiential learning in reflective practice.

Such acceptances of thought and experience can decrease thought and experience suppression while increasing dispositional openness, a trait characterized by curiosity and receptivity to new experiences (McCrae & Costa, 1987).

In other words, practitioners of mindfulness are trained to see "the bright side" of their experiences, reconceptualizing their feelings and experiences regarding events that may have once been viewed as negative and stressful.

THE HISTORICAL UNDERPINNINGS OF MINDFULNESS

Origins. The most popular use of the term "mindfulness" is derived from the eastern contemplative Buddhist practice. Pali was the language of Buddhist psychology 2,500 years ago, and mindfulness is the core teaching of this tradition, the term itself a translation of the Pali word *sati* that connotes awareness, attention, and remembering (Germer, Siegel, & Fulton, 2013). *Sati*, or mindfulness, is also one of the seven factors in enlightenment, with techniques deeply rooted in Buddhist traditions.

The spread of mindfulness concepts to Western culture can be traced as far back as the 1800s, when the writings of D. T. Suzuki boosted the popularity of Zen Buddhism by adjusting it to Western tastes. Despite its religious origins, though, most mindfulness skills are now taught without reference to their religious roots, making it more universally acceptable as a disciplinary practice (Hayes & Wilson, 2003).

Increasingly, mindfulness has been viewed as an acceptable and distinct mechanism by which to monitor and manage one's emotions. In 1979, Jon Kabat-Zinn founded the Mindfulness-Based Stress Reduction (MBSR) program at the University of Massachusetts to treat people with chronic illnesses. The program sparked the application of mindfulness ideas and practices for the treatment of a variety of conditions in both healthy and unhealthy people.

Today, MBSR (stress reduction) programs are used around the world in an array of fields and locations, including hospitals, schools, and rehabilitation centers. Physicians and medical practitioners have become particularly interested in using MBSR as a means to heal or self-regulate personal stressors that are outside of the patients' control (Langer & Moldoveanu, 2000).

These techniques have proven to be beneficial in raising patients' self-awareness, thereby helping them modify to their lifestyle behaviors and to take greater responsibility for their life choices (Ruff & Mackenzie, 2009). Mindfulness practice is also being employed in psychology to assist with issues like anxiety, obsessive-compulsive disorder, and even drug addiction.

MINDFULNESS IN EDUCATIONAL LEADERSHIP

As noted, educational leaders work in stressful environments that require them to make difficult, high-stakes decisions throughout their day. Their jobs also press them to engage in many crucial conversations, which can be equally stressful. Mindfulness practices include activities such as deep breathing and meditation that can help school leaders to alleviate and even avoid some of their stress associated with tough decision-making, vision-making and having crucial conversations.

Another component of mindful behavior is to remain present—or in the moment—which can facilitate clearer thinking for decision-making. As such, school leaders practicing mindfulness are completely focused on the present so that they make sound, thoughtful decisions. Improved communication is also an added benefit of mindfulness, as those communicating with a principal—who is fully present—feel heard and valued.

Principals who practice mindfulness can create a school culture that promotes mindfulness in their teachers. They realize that teachers can also benefit from dispositions obtained through mindfulness practice as they too work under similarly stressful conditions and are charged with communicating with a variety of challenging personalities as well.

Frank, Reibel, Broderick, Cantrell, and Metz (2015) conducted a study of teachers who engaged in MBSR and learned that mindfulness practice promoted educator's personal and professional well-being.

The teachers in this study completed an eight-week MBSR program delivered by a certified MBSR instructor. Teachers were taught mindfulness practices that included body scan, awareness of breathing, mindful yoga, eating meditation, and walking meditation. Teachers benefited from improved self-compassion, self-kindness, and mindfulness. However, the most significant improvement experienced by teachers in this study was improved sleep quality (Frank et al., 2015). Mindfulness practice clearly benefits people from a variety of professions and walks of life in multiple ways.

Corporate leader, Bill George (2012), had an opportunity to meet with the Dalai Lama, and asked him what it took to become an authentic leader. To this, Dalai Lama replied, "You must have practices you engage in every day." George had the following to say of how mindfulness practice enhanced his experience as a leader:

> My most important introspective practice is meditation. . . . In 1975, I went with my wife to a Transcendental Meditation (TM) Workshop. Although I never adopted the spiritual portion of TM, the physical practice became part of my daily routine. Meditation has been a Godsend for me. As an active leader who has held highly stressful roles since my mid-twenties, I was diagnosed with high blood pressure in my thirties.
>
> When I started meditating, I was able to stay calmer and more focused on my leadership, without losing the "edge" that I believed had made me successful. Meditation caused me to cast off the many trivial worries that once possessed me and gain clarity about what was really important. I gradually became more

self-aware and more sensitive to the impact that I was having on others. Just as important, my blood pressure returned to normal and stayed there. (2012, pp. 30–31)

George learned about a practice that not only made him more aware of how his interactions impacted others but he also became a healthier person overall who was able to think more clearly. This type of clarity and focus is needed by school leaders to become effective decision-makers and leaders, as well as to stay physically and emotionally healthy enough to work well in school leadership without early burnout. Kearney, Kelsey, and Herrington (2013) found that in addition to improved health outcomes and student performance, mindfulness in school leaders also contributed to student achievement and student success.

In their research, Kearney et al. (2013) conducted a mixed-methods study in which they employed Hoy's inventory (M-scale) and found that principals' mindfulness made a statistically significant independent contribution to the variance in the outcome measure. In this study, student success rate was measured by a combination of students' passing rates on competency-based tests in reading and math in the state of Texas, and the percentage of students receiving commended performance acknowledgments in math for the year in which this study was conducted.

Commended performance is defined by the Texas education agency and is above the required standard. A qualitative study, followed by Hoy's M-scale inventory, was conducted to question principals and their staff who scored highest in mindfulness; and three themes emerged from this part of the study. Mindful principals were found to try new things, often to build relationships and to practice reflection—and the practice of reflection was used toward continuous improvement of leadership practice.

Relationship building and the practice of reflection toward improvement of leadership are both obvious benefits of mindfulness for effective leadership. Mindfulness is effective in helping to alleviate stress, as noted earlier. Sauer and Kohls (2011) further found that mindfulness was also beneficial for a variety of psychological symptoms such as distress, anxiety, and depression. It is also beneficial for alleviating psycho-physiological variables such as pain, sleep quality, immune parameters, and allocation of attention resources (p. 294).

Perhaps the most compelling reasons for engaging in mindfulness might be for its benefits to the brain. Research finding shows that mindfulness practitioners had greater gray matter proportions in the parts of the brain where mindfulness is practiced. Further, mindfulness meditation proved to strengthen the working memory and to reduce the decline associated with normal aging. This fact should be especially compelling to educators who recognize the power of the brain as the epicenter of all physical and mental activity, as well as the source of all creativity.

REFLECTIVE PRACTICE AND MINDFULNESS: UNLIKELY BEDFELLOWS

Reflective practice and mindfulness practices appear to be opposing practices on the surface. Reflective practice calls for practitioners to spend time reflecting upon actions previously taken. Leaders are thus to muse over their previous actions with the purpose of understanding why they committed the actions they did—and how their actions impacted others. On the other hand, mindfulness advocates for practitioners to remain in the moment and to focus 100 percent in the present moment. Mindfulness instruction even includes teaching that appears antireflective.

And too much focus on what has already transpired is referred to as *rumination*, which is thought to be counterproductive. Rumination can cause one to be regretful of the past and to become stuck in regret rather than positively progressing forward. Another belief—which is seemingly conflicting between mindfulness practice and reflective practice—is that mindfulness requires practitioners to be nonjudgmental.

This nonjudgmental aspect of mindfulness refers to not being judgmental of what is presently occurring as one is in the present moment, rather than past occurrences that should be evaluated during reflective practice, whereas reflective practice requires practitioners to reflect and to evaluate previous performance—which could, on the surface, be viewed as judging.

The idea behind reflection, however, is to learn from previous performance with the purpose of improving future performance. Therefore, reflection can be employed positively toward this end. Reflection fits into the meditation portion of mindfulness practice. Meditators can incorporate thoughts of improving their professional performance prior to their entering deeper levels of meditation, which call for clearer thoughts. Practitioners of mindfulness should regularly engage in meditation. Advanced practitioners meditate up to several times a day, and for extended periods of time. Others may start or end their day with a brief meditation.

Another feature shared by reflective practice and mindfulness is that they can be difficult skills to acquire; and both reflective practice and mindfulness, therefore, require time, focused thinking, and effort. Both reflective practice and mindfulness practice can be taught on levels from rudimentary to expert levels. An example of how mindfulness can start off on a rudimentary level—and move to more formal activity—is learning to be mindful while brushing

Improving Student Outcomes through Reflective Practice 59

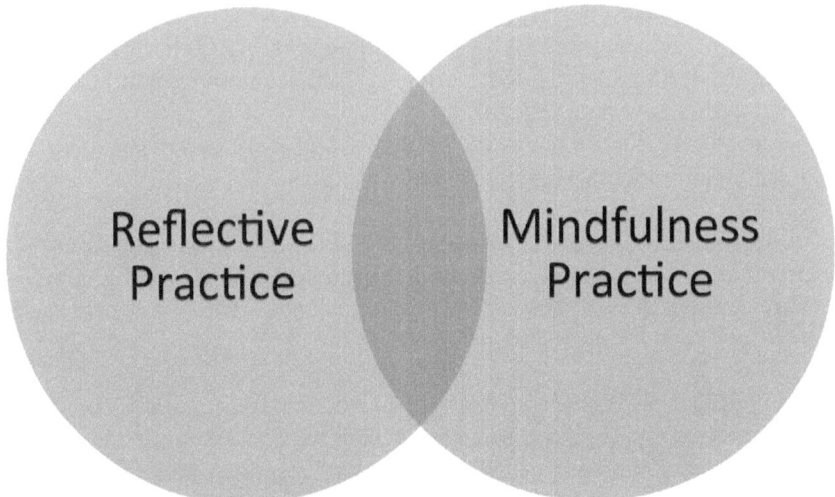

Figure 5.1. Key Practices in Social Life

teeth or waiting for the bus. Or it can be as simple as concentrating on posture while sitting.

Thus, more formal manifestations of mindfulness include systematic and deliberate actions, such as (a) focusing on breaths, slow and conscious walking; (b) fostering what we perceive through our senses; and (c) deliberately sorting out of mental evaluations, comments, and prejudices. This sorting can also be classified as reflectivity.

One does not become reflective or mindful without rehearsal and intentionality. In fact, reflective practice and mindfulness are lifestyle choices. Although I attempted to make reflective practice and mindfulness appear as an essential part of successful leadership practice, it is still the choice of the practitioner to adopt these practices and to include the tools of reflective practice and mindfulness in their individual toolboxes, unless employers require their practitioners to employ these strategies. See figure 5.1.

IMPLICATIONS FOR EDUCATIONAL LEADERS AND LEADERSHIP PREPARATION PROGRAMS

Making time for reflective practice and mindfulness is difficult for educational leaders unless their practice is very deliberate. School leaders find themselves so bogged down with demanding day-to-day responsibilities of school management that they do only what they feel is absolutely essential to their survival. Many principals would argue that they do not have time to practice mindfulness, but Hedberg argues that they do not have the luxury of neglecting this important practice.

Hedberg (2009) emphasizes the importance of reflective practice, stating that neglecting reflective practice is not wise. She explains,

> Viewing reflective practice as an afterthought, or worse, as an extravagance few can afford, leaves out an essential part of managerial learning. Consequently, it becomes essential to deliberately and purposefully build reflective thought into the cognitive repertoire of our students. (p. 11)

Hedberg (2009) places the responsibility of teaching the importance of reflective practice on leadership preparation programs. She recognizes how busy leaders will become, once placed in their positions, advocates for reflection to be built into leadership training. Hedberg further notes,

> A cultural push for active work and being busy makes reflection a luxury that few of our students indulge. For this reason, it becomes even more important for management educators to teach our students why they might want to be reflective practitioners and to give them skills in building their own reflective practice.... The classroom can be a wonderful place for reflective learning.... The classroom is a place not only where analyses occur and actions get taken, but where managers can gain the perspective needed to see general patterns, ponder alternative actions, be aware of consequences, learn how others might perceive the situation differently, and challenge assumptions about what needs to be done. (2009, p. 12)

In short, the first implication from this work is that leadership programs should incorporate training in reflective and mindfulness practice. Although aspects of mindfulness practice and reflective practice must be learned in the context of day-to-day work, educational leadership students, who work full or part-time, are able to see the implication for their practices immediately and can share their experiences with their mindfulness and reflective practices in class for the benefit of other students.

Students with fewer on-the-job experiences can learn from in-class case studies and the resulting questions that the instructor might ask to teach reflection and mindfulness strategies in the classroom setting. See figure 5.2.

The second implication to be noted is that although mindfulness and reflective practice begin with the school leader, the entire school can benefit from mindfulness. This process would require principals becoming versed in reflective and mindfulness practices, and implementing policies that reinforce these practices as well as high-quality ongoing professional development for

Improving Student Outcomes through Reflective Practice

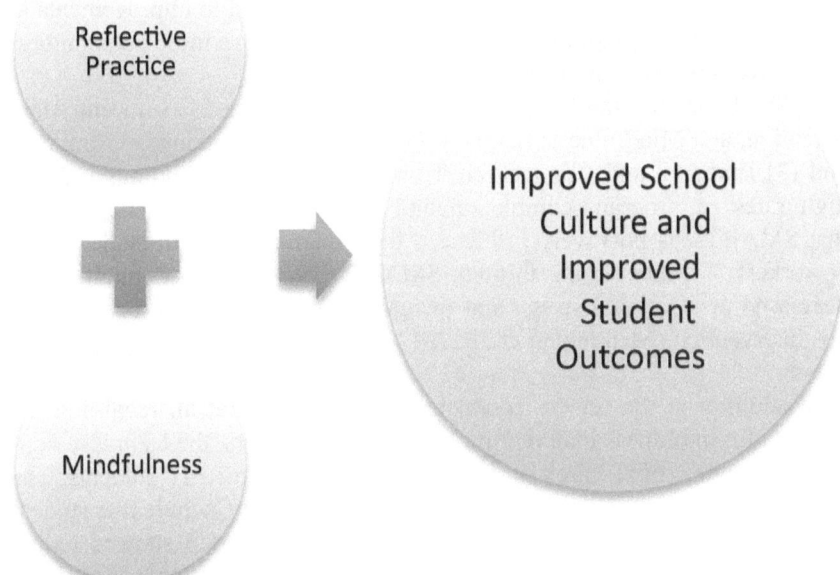

Figure 5.2. Two Means to Better Schools and Outcomes

teachers. Teachers would also need to be given the time and space to employ reflection and mindfulness in their curricula and classroom culture.

Burrows's (2011) work reinforces the need for mindfulness and notes that social and emotional competence is necessary to help educators to respond properly to the emotional challenges of classroom and school environments. Burrows further postulates that relational mindfulness—an approach that facilitates listening to ourselves and others by integrating mindfulness with Western counseling skills—has the potential to assist educators in maintaining equanimity in intense classroom and school environments.

Meiklejohn et al. (2012) review mindfulness training for teachers and students and find overwhelmingly positive impacts. Researchers note that Mindfulness Based Wellness Education benefits teachers by providing them with more tools for their toolboxes, thus improving the quality of education overall.

Cultivating Awareness and Resilience in Education (CARE) and Stress Management and Relaxation Techniques (SMART) in education are discussed. Both mindfulness-based programs improved teacher's performance and well-being. CARE has four aims, including (1) to improve teachers' overall well-being; (2) to improve teachers' effectiveness in providing emotional, behavioral, and instructional support to students; (3) to improve teacher-child relationships; and (4) to increase students' prosocial behavior.

Preliminary studies illustrate promising results related to improvements in teachers' levels of mindfulness, well-being, and in using a more autonomous, supportive motivational orientation in the classroom.

SMART includes the following three sets of elements: (1) Concentration, Attention, and Mindfulness; (2) Awareness and Understanding of Emotions; and (3) Empathy and Compassion Training. Preliminary findings indicate high rates of program completion and satisfaction; and teachers report that SMART has positively influenced their interactions with students and coworkers. Teachers going through SMART report increased mindfulness, decreased occupational stress, and increased work motivation from pre- to postintervention (Meiklejohn et al., 2012, p. 295, cited in Jennings et al., in press).

In addition to the review conducted by Meiklejohn et al. regarding the impact of mindfulness intervention programs on teachers, the team also conducted a review of research on teaching mindfulness to K–12 students. The studies reviewed were numerous; however, key findings include that student participants who attended the Attention Academy Program showed reductions in test anxiety and improvements in teacher-rated attention, social skills, and objective measures of selective attention (Napoli et al., 2005).

Other studies of elementary- and middle-school–aged children found improvements in attention and academic performance, less anxiety, reductions in behavioral and anger management problems, as noted by parent reports, and improved sleep quality. Studies conducted upon high school students found improvements in working memory, sleep, reduced worry and mental distress, and reduced state and trait anxiety; and teacher ratings showed improvements of students' social skills, problem behaviors, and academics.

The health benefits and social-emotional implications noted previously make it clear that mindfulness not only benefits the school leader but also potentially teachers, students, and parents as well. Mindful and reflective teachers would run more effective classrooms; and mindful and reflective students would be able to focus and work harder to perform at higher levels on end of grade (EOG) and standards-based examinations. And incidences where discipline referrals had been an issue would likely decline, as these students would also be less prone to violent or disruptive behavior.

Teachers, students, and parents alike can benefit from reflective practice and mindfulness practice. The culture of a mindful school would naturally demand less violence stoppage and increased academic performance, based upon the said benefits of both reflective practice and mindfulness practice. As principals master the art of reflective and mindfulness practices, they too should endeavor to run mindful schools.

REFERENCES

Bishop, S. R., et al. (2004). Mindfulness: A Proposed Operational Definition. *Clinical psychology: Science and practice. 11:3* pp. 225–341.
Boud, D., Keogh, R., & Walker, D. (1985). *Reflection: Turning experience into learning.* London: Kogan Page. [add Boud in text.] *Adult Education Quarterly, 61*(2), 181–197.
Burrows, L. (2011). Relational mindfulness in education. *Encounter: Education for Meaning and Social Justice, 24*(4), 24–29.
Bush, T. (2009). Leadership development and school improvement: Contemporary issues in leadership development. *Educational review, 61*(4), 375–389.
Dewey, J. (1933). *How we think.* Lexington, MA: D.C. Heath.
Frank, J. L., Reibel, D., Broderick, P., Cantrell, T., & Metz, S. (2015). The effectiveness of mindfulness-based stress reduction on educator stress and well-being: Results from a pilot study. *Mindfulness, 6*(2), 208–216.
George, B. (2012). Mindfulness helps you become a better leader. *Harvard Business Review, 26,* 21–32.
Germer, C. (2004). What is mindfulness? Insight Journal. Fall, pp. 24–29.
Germer, C. K., Siegel, R. D., & Fulton, P. R. (2013). Mindfulness and Psychotherapy. New York: The Guilford Press.
Hayes, S. C., & Wilson, K. G. (2003). Mindfulness: Method and process. *Clinical Psychology: Science and Practice, 10,* 161–165.
Hedberg, P. R. (2009). Learning through reflective classroom practice: Applications to educate the reflective manager. *Journal of Management Education, 33*(1), 10–36.
Jordi, R. (2011). Reframing the Concept of Reflection: Consciousness, Experiential Learning, and Reflective Learning Practices. *Adult Education Quarterly, 61*(2), 181–197.
Kabat-Zinn, J. (1990). *Full catastrophe living.* New York: Bantam Doubleday Dell Publishing Group.
Kearney, W. S., Kelsey, C., & Herrington, D. (2013). Mindful leaders in highly effective schools: A mixed-method application of Hoy's M-scale. *Educational Management Administration & Leadership, 41*(3), 316–335.
Klee, S., & Garfinkel, B. (1983). The computerized continuous performance test: A new measure of inattention. *Journal of Abnormal Psychology, 11,* 487–496.
Langer, E. J. (1989). *Mindfulness.* Boston: Addison-Wesley.
Langer, E. J., & Moldoveanu, M. (2000). The Society for the Psychological Study of Social Issues: Mindfulness Research and the Future. *Journal of Social Issues, 56,* 129–139.
Leithwood, Kenneth, Day, Christopher, Sammons. C. Pam., Harris, Alma, & Hopkins, David (2006). Successful School Leadership: What It Is and How It Influences Pupil." Research Report. University of Nottingham, England.
McCrae, R. R., & Costa, P. T. (1987). Validation of the five-factor model of personality across instruments and observers. *Journal of Personality and Social Psychology, 52*(1), 81–90.

McCabe, R. K., & Mackenzie, E. R. (2009). The role of mindfulness in healthcare reform: A policy paper. Explore (NY). Nov–Dec; 5(6), 313–323.

Meiklejohn, J., Phillips, C., Freedman, M. L., Griffin, M. L., Biegel, G., Roach, A., & Isberg, R. (2012). Integrating mindfulness training into K–12 education: Fostering the resilience of teachers and students. *Mindfulness, 3*(4), 291–307.

Osterman, K. F., & Kottkamp, R. B. (1993). *Reflective practice for educators.* Newbury Park, CL: Corwin Press.

Osterman, K. F., & Kottkamp, R. B. (1993), Reflective Practice for Educators: Improving Schooling Through Professional Development. Newbury Park, CA: Corwin Press.

Rogers T & Monsell, 1995 and in cognitive inhibition (Bishop et al., 2004).

Schon, D. A. (1983). *The Reflective Practitioner: How professionals think in action.* New York: Basic Books.

Vince, R., & Reynolds, M. (2004). Organizing reflective practice. *Management & Learning, 33*(1), 63–78.

Walker, A., & Qian, H. (2006). Beginning principals: Balancing at the top of the greasy pole. *Journal of Educational Administration, 44*(4), 297–309.

Chapter 6

Visionary Leadership for Diversity in K–12 Schools: Looking Back to Move Forward

Floyd D. Beachum and Carlos R. McCray

W. E. B. DuBois (2008) insightfully noted that the problem of the twentieth century would be the color line. This was the line that racially divided the real lived experiences of different peoples. While DuBois (2008) was primarily referring to the line between whites and blacks, the twentieth century would highlight examples of extreme intolerance and oppression enforced on multiple groups.

The twentieth century would also bear witness to the struggle for women to receive the right to vote as well as be integrated into the workplace; it spawned two world wars that emerged from the seeds of nationalism, imperialism, prejudice, and brinkmanship; it witnessed the horrors and genocide of the Holocaust; and it included a long and bloody struggle for civil rights and economic equity in the United States, to name a few.

All of these examples highlight instances of difference that could have benefitted from a deeper understanding and appreciation of diversity. As we go further into the twenty-first century, will the United States "dedicate itself to" or "deter from" its diverse destiny? Cox (2001) wrote, "the stakes are high, especially in countries like the United States that feature high levels of cultural diversity, a democratic political tradition, and legal and value systems that place great emphasis on fairness, respect, and equal opportunity" (p. 16). The place where these messages are either reinforced or rejected is in American schools. For in schools, we learn to read, write, respond, relate, recount, and come to different realizations. According to Gordon (2006):

> Without question, education is the key to progress and prosperity in the United States today. Whether fair or not, educational opportunity and academic achievement are directly tied to the social divisions associated with race, ethnicity, gender, first language, and social class. The level and quality of educational attainment either open doors to opportunity or close them. (p. 25)

Thus, American schools can play a key role in not only academic preparation of its citizens but also crucial life opportunities and outcomes. For education for diversity needs visionary leadership, which is the main premise of this chapter.

Our task in this chapter is to develop and articulate a *vision for diversity* for leadership in schools. We start by recognizing the need to address changing demographic patterns as rationale for a diversity-based vision. Then, we ground the vision in ethical principles that reinforce America's greater democratic values. Next, we utilize a reflective analysis to gain insight from some of our previous works in an effort then to use that information to formulate a future vision for diversity. Finally, we discuss implications for leadership preparation and practice in schools.

EDUCATIONAL CONTEXT FOR DIVERSITY DEMOGRAPHIC CHANGE

The United States of America is continuing a trend of greater demographic change, especially within K–12 schools. A 2016 report commissioned by *The Century Foundation* indicated:

> This report argues that, as our K–12 student population becomes more racially and ethnically diverse, the time is right for our political leaders to pay more attention to the evidence, intuition, and common sense that supports the importance of racially and ethnically diverse educational settings to prepare the next generation. It highlights in particular the large body of research that demonstrates the important educational benefits—cognitive, social, and emotional—for all students who interact with classmates from different backgrounds, cultures, and orientations to the world. (Wells, Fox, & Cordova-Cabo, 2016, p. 4)

The aforementioned statements are not just for political leaders but also for educational leaders as well. Demographic changes in school inevitably affect school culture, discipline procedures, teaching strategies, and relationships and outcomes/learning (McCray & Beachum, 2014a). An article from The Center for Public Education (CPE) identified at least five demographic trends that are impacting public education:

1. The U.S. population is getting older.
2. The U.S. population is growing more diverse.
3. The U.S. population is growing older and more diverse at the same time.
4. The U.S. population as a whole is growing rapidly.
5. The West and South are growing more quickly than the Northeast and Midwest (Crouch & Zakariya, 2012).

The implication is that the population of the United States is growing older and more diverse socially and economically with the demographic changes more pronounced in certain geographical areas. Because of immigration patterns and births according to race/ethnicity, the population changes tend to start on the East and West coasts and the Southwest United States (Hodgkinson, 1998).

These demographic changes slowly spread into the rest of the country and inevitably have an impact on schools. Villegas and Lucas (2002) wrote, "While children of color constituted about one-third of the student population in 1995, they are expected to become the numerical majority by 2035. This change will render the expression 'minority students' statistically inaccurate" (p. 3).

Specifically, students of color will make up large percentages of the student body in many school districts—and educators should be prepared to deal with differences in culture, language, income, and perspectives. According to McCray, Beachum, and Yawn (2012),

> These educators deal with context-specific, complex situations that are rife with issues of diversity, professional ethics, and moral dilemmas as major topic or subtle subtext. Therefore, more nuanced ways of dealing with diverse populations, mediating issues between individuals who have vastly different approaches toward educational success, and ensuring an equitable educational environment, are critical components of 21st-century schools. (p. 92)

This will require educators who are prepared to engage more diverse student bodies and communities.

ETHICAL IMPERATIVE

While the demographic rationale for a visionary leadership for diversity is compelling, this effort also includes an ethical imperative. This move is supported by the simple notion that leadership for diversity is the right thing to do effectively to serve all student populations. This mentality is forever solidified in some of America's most treasured documents and recitations. Two examples include the Preamble to the Constitution of the United States and the Pledge of Allegiance. The Preamble to the U.S. Constitution reads:

> We the People of the United States, in Order to form a more perfect Union, establish Justice, insure domestic Tranquility, provide for the common defense, promote the general Welfare, and secure the Blessings of Liberty to ourselves and our Posterity, do ordain and establish this Constitution for the United States of America.

One will note that the wording includes "establish justice," "promote the general Welfare," and "secure the Blessings of Liberty." The reference to justice guarantees fairness, and educational leaders should lead and make decisions in a fair and equitable manner. Promoting the general welfare supports the notion that the government will take care of all its citizens as much as possible.

Similarly, leaders for diversity should promote the general welfare of the people whom they lead, creating effective environments where people can maximize their talents and potential. The phrase "secure the Blessings of Liberty" protects U.S. citizens from unjust laws and tyranny. For visionary leaders, they too should strive to respect the freedom given by liberty—and balance that with job expectations and work demands when dealing with subordinates.

The Pledge of Allegiance reads: "I pledge allegiance to the Flag of the United States of America, and to the Republic for which it stands, one Nation under God, indivisible, with liberty and justice for all."

One will note again the reference to liberty and justice. These are the reoccurring, powerful themes in the establishment and continuation of the American democratic social experiment. Therefore, they should not be relegated only to our most prized documentation and one of our most-memorized recitations.

These concepts should permeate the social fabric of our nation and be reflected in the essence of our organizations. Thus, visionary leadership for diversity strives to make organizational cultures more effective, receptive, engaging, and truly multicultural through the actions of leaders (Cox, 2001).

The ethical imperative for visionary diversity leadership can be recognized by the lofty language of liberty, justice, and equality; but it can be more difficult to grasp in everyday reality. To be a leader usually means to have and use a certain amount of power or authority. Unfortunately, some leaders misuse their power and bend it to their own benefit. Instead, an ethical mindset recognizes equal respect in organizations. According to Strike, Haller, and Soltis (1998), "We cannot treat people as though they were things, mere objects, who are valued only insofar as they contribute to our welfare. We must consider their welfare as well. People cannot be treated as though they were nothing more than instruments to serve our purposes" (p. 17).

This approach recognizes people's individuality and identities, which shows respect (Tatum, 1997). It rejects a color-blind approach that while recognizing people's humanity can avoid the difficulty of addressing the individuality of a person's culture, background, customs, perspective, and worldview (McCray & Beachum, 2014b; Milner, 2010; Villegas & Lucas, 2002).

Hence, a vision for diversity—undergirded by a connection to ethical principals in practice—can provide greater leadership clarity and not fall prey to the dimness of a color-blind mind-set. Beachum and McCray (2010) stated, "This reinforces and does not refute the American ideals of life, liberty, and the pursuit of happiness *for all*. Recognizing diversity makes us moral members of a concerned community that seeks to realize great ideological pursuits such as equality and democracy" (pp. 207–208). Thus, recognition of diversity can better align leadership perspectives with broader democratic principles.

HINDSIGHT AS FORESIGHT

For the creation of our vision, we will reflect back on some of our previous diversity-related scholarship. These works are representative of our combined perspective on issues of leadership, equity, equality, social justice, urban education, and multicultural education. We limit the works to only articles or book chapters (no books) (see table 6.1). In the following section, we will briefly describe the major ideas in each of these works, analyzing them

Table 6.1. Diversity Related Publications

Publication Title	Journal	Publication Type	Authors/Date	Audience/ Orientation
1. Cultural Collision in Urban Schools	Current Issues in Education	Article	Beachum & McCray (2004)	Academics, practitioners
2. Capital Matters: A Pedagogy of Self-Development: Making Room for Alternative Forms of Capital	Contemporary Perspectives on Capital in Educational Context	Book chapter	McCray & Beachum (2011)	Academics
3. The Fast and the Serious: Exploring the Notion of Culturally Relevant Leadership	African American Students in Urban Schools: Critical Issues and Solutions for Achievement	Book chapter	Beachum & McCray (2012)	Academics
4. Exploring the Intersectionality of Multiple Centers within Notions of Social Justice	Journal of School Leadership	Article	Dantley, Beachum, & McCray (2008)	Academics, practitioners

for broader concepts. We will then synthesize these broader concepts into a framework for diversity-based visionary leadership.

CULTURAL COLLISION AND COLLUSION

The terms *cultural collision* and *cultural collusion* were based on some of our early works. It began with an article in the journal *Current Issues in Education*. Cultural collision is a clash in cultures, values, and/or beliefs (Beachum & McCray, 2004), especially between the cultures of vulnerable students and middle-class educators (Beachum & McCray, 2011). We would later include the notion of cultural collusion, which is when the same vulnerable students do not fully engage in their own learning (not giving enough effort, not completing assignments, being nonchalant about their education, etc.).

At the same time, educators may also not do anything extra to reach or encourage these students. Thus, both groups (students and educators) have colluded in an implicit agreement that ultimately fails the student. Cultural collision and collusion are grounded in other similar works. Dyson (1997) wrote about "juvenocracies," which are areas controlled by primarily black and Latino youth under the age of twenty-five who assume financial, psychological, and physical influence. By applying this definition to the rules and routines of school, we were able to develop the concepts of cultural collision and collusion.

Cultural collision and collusion can be examined for a deeper insight into visionary leadership for diversity. Cultural collision recognizes that students can come from a variety of different cultural backgrounds. The school on the other hand has the responsibility to meet students where they are and educate them properly no matter their race/ethnicity, primary language, ability status, or socioeconomic situation (Beachum & McCray, 2016; Capper & Frattura, 2009).

Cultural collusion lets educators know that they have the greater responsibility to do everything in their power to reach and teach their students, not letting them fall through the cracks and fall into academic failure or drop out altogether (Balfanz & Byrnes, 2012; Delpit, 1995). Recognizing cultural collision requires a kind of *insight* into diversity, and addressing cultural collusion requires *extra effort*.

PEDAGOGY OF SELF-DEVELOPMENT

The pedagogy of self-development appeared as an insightful framework as part of a chapter in the book *Contemporary Perspectives on Capital in*

Educational Contexts (Bartee, 2011). For students, it highlights self-realization and self-assertion along with the recognition of relevant forms of capital (Yosso, 2005). McCray and Beachum (2011) indicated:

> Self-realization contains the elements of familial, resistant, and linguistic capital. These three forms of capital are helpful as students formulate goals, careers, and dreams for the future. Self-assertion encompasses aspirational, social, and navigational capital. These forms of capital address how students cope with others, operate in society, and develop resiliency. This framework has insightful implications for teachers and school leaders. (p. 94)

For teachers and school leaders, the pedagogy of self-development recognizes the real lived experiences of students (especially students of color) and not stereotypes or misperception. It can provide a counter-narrative or more authentic reality for educators who may explicitly or implicitly undervalue or underserve these students (Perry, 2003; Prier, 2012). This framework illuminates the idea of *agency* in students.

CULTURALLY RELEVANT LEADERSHIP

Culturally relevant leadership is informed by the work of Ladson-Billings (1994, 1995), where she explored culturally relevant pedagogy. Culturally relevant teachers had a passion for teaching and learning, promoted equity in their classrooms, and took responsibility for the academic success of all of their students. Culturally relevant leadership is based on the tenets of liberatory consciousness, pluralistic insight, and reflexive practice. A comprehensive examination of this concept appeared in the book *African American Students in Urban Schools: Critical Issues and Solutions for Achievement* (Moore & Lewis, 2012). McCray and Beachum (2014a) wrote:

> CRL can be applied as a process not only for the self-edification of school leaders, but also in certain situations where the school leader is dealing with a specific problem or challenge. This enables the leader who is using CRL to (1) challenge their current thinking by observing alternatives and gaining additional information (liberatory consciousness); (2) examine their true feelings and attitude about the topic at hand and its impact on all students (pluralistic insight); and (3) take action and engage in practices that are equitable, morally informed and reflective in nature (reflexive practice). (p. 408)

Culturally Relevant Leadership recognizes *self-examination, an affirming attitude, and pragmatism.*

SOCIAL JUSTICE LEADERSHIP

In a special issue of the *Journal of School Leadership*, we wrote an article titled, "Exploring the Intersectionality of Multiple Centers within Notions of Social Justice" (Dantley, Beachum, & McCray, 2008). In this study, we stated that social justice—while a worthy and noble goal—is vulnerable to being co-opted (people say social justice just to be relevant or trendy), myopic (people are primarily concerned with their own area of interest, such as gender, race/ethnicity, social class), or being too theoretical and not practical. Young (1990) also articulated another aspect about the issues within social justice:

> The ideal of the just society as eliminating group differences is both unrealistic and undesirable. Instead justice in a group-differentiated society demands social equality of groups, and mutual recognition and affirmation of group differences. Attending to group-specific needs and providing for group representation both promotes that social equality and provides the recognition that undermines cultural imperialism. (p. 191)

In response, we asserted that social justice leadership should be relationship-driven, holistic, and morally based. Pedagogically, we sought to offer *alternative discourses*, encourage *interdisciplinary classroom approaches*, and encourage a more *adaptive approach* to decision-making.

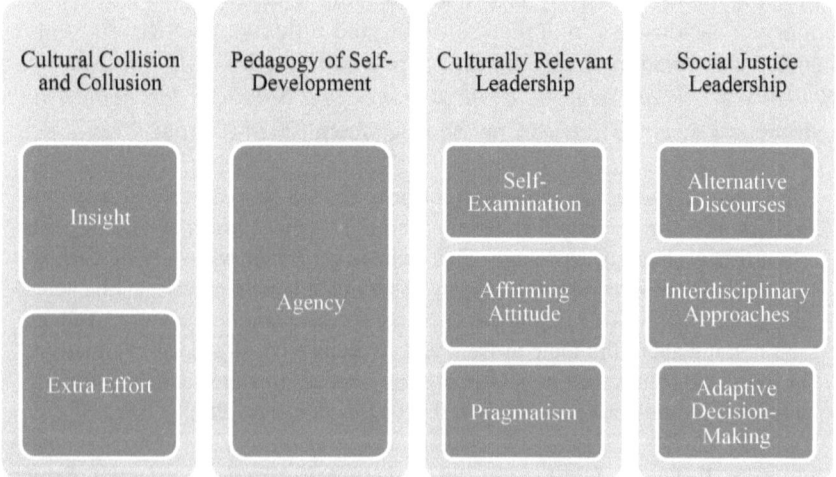

Figure 6.1. **The Elements of a Leadership Vision for Diversity**

Table 6.2. Leadership Vision for Diversity

Introspection	Empowerment
Self-examination	Agency
Affirming attitude	Alternative discourses
Insight	Interdisciplinary approaches
Extra effort	Adaptive decision-making
	Pragmatism

DEVELOPING A NEW LEADERSHIP VISION FOR DIVERSITY

The new vision for diversity leadership we are advocating here is a result of looking back over thirteen years of related scholarship. The elements of this vision can be seen in figure 6.1.

While these elements are helpful, they can be further synthesized into broader concepts. Self-examination, affirming attitude, insight, and extra effort can all be related to personal leadership attributes, qualities, or perspectives, which can be titled, *introspection*. And agency, alternative discourses, interdisciplinary approaches, adaptive decision-making, and pragmatism can all be labeled as *empowerment* activities. Therefore, a vision for leadership in the area of diversity should involve both introspection and empowerment (see table 6.2).

INTROSPECTION

Introspection is inward-looking and acknowledges that visionary leaders need first to look at themselves in dealing with issues of diversity. This effort starts with self-examination, which forces a leader to do self-inquiry asking themselves questions about what they believe about different people, how they are impacted by bias, and what they can do to gain new knowledge (Beachum & McCray, 2016; Milner, 2006; Ryan, 2006).

In dealing with diversity, leaders should have an affirming attitude toward various people across all of their social identities (race/ethnicity, gender, social class, first language, ability status, etc.). This is important because attitudes can influence actions (Tatum, 2007). Once leaders have looked inward and have the proper mind-set, they should also mentally prepare to give an extra effort to make their goals a realization in the area of promoting diversity—and thus building better organizations (Cox, 2001; McCray & Beachum, 2014b).

EMPOWERMENT

The second component of the vision shifts the focus toward areas external to the leader. Agency is the ability to act for oneself. It begins the process of changing the outside world by first having leaders recognize that they personally are primary agents of change (Beachum, 2015; Fullan, 2004; Kouzes & Posner, 2007). Those leaders for diversity are change leaders (Cox, 2001) who may have to promote alternative discourses, meaning that they may have to be the dissenting voice or stand up for nonpopular decisions or perspectives. In education, these leaders also see the inherent value of interdisciplinary approaches.

They understand that one field of study is not stagnant, isolated, or paramount; they can be informed by other fields. For instance, educational leadership can draw from fields like history, law, and sociology. Adaptive decision-making is a necessary skill for leaders in this era. This is a necessity in this time where problems are complex and multifaceted (Fullan, 2004). Lastly, leaders for diversity should understand that their approaches need to be pragmatic. The true value of a vision is measured by the ability for it to be put into action (West, 2008).

RECOMMENDATIONS AND CONCLUSION

The aforementioned leadership vision for diversity has the potential to inform leadership preparation and school leadership practice. In leadership preparation programs more emphasis can be placed on the issue of diversity due to the changing demographic population of the United States. Furthermore, if we understand that the nation is changing, we have an ethical duty to make sure that our school leaders are prepared to interact with and engage diverse communities (Brooks, 2012; McCray & Beachum, 2014a).

These programs should also emphasize the major vision components of introspection and empowerment as well as the elements under each category. In school leadership practice, these elements will be needed in day-to-day diversity-based situations and equitable decisions that administrators might face. In cultivating this vision for diversity, we should consider the words of McCray and Beachum (2014a):

> The state of American education today is one that has resulted from our collective past, policies, and decisions. Seldom are the solutions simple to educational problems and too many times there are various complexities that characterize different sides of educational issues. K–12 schooling's trajectory is one of progression and regression, gains and losses, tremendous strides and difficult lapses. Much of this is centered on issues of diversity. (p. xvi)

REFERENCES

Balfanz, R., & Byrnes, V. (2012). *The importance of being in school: A report on absenteeism in the nation's public schools.* Retrieved from John Hopkins University School of Education Everyone Graduates Center website: http://new.every1graduates.org/wp-content/uploads/2012/05/FINALChronicAbsenteeismReport_May16.pdf

Bartee, R. D. (Ed.). (2011). *Contemporary perspectives on capital in educational contexts.* Charlotte, NC: Information Age Publishing.

Beachum F. D., & McCray, C. R. (2004). Cultural collision in urban schools. *Current Issues in Education* [on-line] 7(5).

Beachum, F. D. (2015). Knowing the truth: The challenge for educational leadership. In A. Pitre, T. G. Allen, & E. Pitre (Eds.), *Multicultural education for educational leaders: Critical race theory and antiracism perspectives* (pp. vii–xi). New York: Rowman and Littlefield.

Beachum, F. D., & McCray, C. M. (2010). Cracking the code: Illuminating the promises and pitfalls of social justice in educational leadership. *International Journal of Urban Educational Leadership*, 4(1), 206–221. Available from: http://www.uc.edu/urbanleadership/current_issues.htm

Beachum, F. D., & McCray, C. R. (2011). *Cultural collision and collusion: Reflections on hip-hop culture, values, and schools.* New York: Peter Lang Publishing.

Beachum, F. D., & McCray, C. R. (2012). The fast and the serious: Exploring the notions of culturally relevant leadership. In J Moore & C. Lewis (Ed.), *Urban school contexts for African American students: Crisis and prospects for Improvement.* New York: Peter Lang.

Beachum, F. D., & McCray, C. R. (2016). Unmasking leadership: African American male scholars' reflections on critique, justice, and caring. In L. Bass (Ed.), *Black masculinity: conceptualizations a framework for Black masculine caring* (pp. 59–76). New York: Peter Lang.

Brooks, J. S. (2012). *Black school, white school: Racism and educational (mis)leadership.* New York: New York. Teachers College Press.

Capper, C. A., & Frattura, E. M. (2009). *Meeting the needs of students of all abilities.* Thousand Oaks: Corwin Press.

Cox, T., Jr. (2001). *Creating the multicultural organization: A strategy for capturing the power of diversity.* San Francisco, CA: Jossey-Bass.

Crouch, R., & Zakariya, S. B. (2012). The United States of education: The changing demographics of the United States and their schools. *Center for Public Education.* Retrieved from: http://www.centerforpubliceducation.org/You-May-Also-Be-Interested-In-landing-page-level/Organizing-a-School-YMABI/The-United-States-of-education-The-changing-demographics-of-the-United-States-and-their-schools.html

Dantley, M., Beachum, F. D., & McCray, C. R. (2008). Exploring the intersectionality of multiple centers within notions of social justice. *Journal of School Leadership*, 18(2), 124–133.

DuBois, W. E. B., & Edwards, B. H. (2008). *The souls of black folk*. New York: Oxford University Press.

Dyson, M. E. (1997). *Race rules: Navigating the color line*. New York: Vintage Books.

Fullan, M. (2004). *Leading in a culture of change: Personal action guide and workbook*. San Francisco, CA: Jossey-Bass.

Gordon, E. W. (2006). Establishing a system of public education in which all children achieve at high levels and reach their full potential. In T. Smiley (Ed.), *The covenant with Black America* (pp. 23–45). Chicago, IL: Third World Press.

Hodgkinson, H. L. (1998). *Predicting demographics in the nation's schools*. Washington, DC: Center for Democratic Policy, Institute for Educational Leadership.

Kouzes, J. M., & Posner, B. Z. (2007). *The leadership challenge* (4th ed.). San Francisco, CA: Jossey-Bass.

Ladson-Billings, G. (1994). *The dreamkeepers: Successful teachers of African-American students*. San Francisco, CA: Jossey-Bass.

Ladson-Billings, G. (1995). But that's just good teaching! The case for culturally relevant pedagogy. *Theory into Practice, 34*, 159–165.

McCray, C. R., & Beachum, F. D. (2014a). Countering plutocracies: Increasing autonomy and accountability through culturally relevant leadership. *The Journal of School Leadership and Management*. doi: 10.1080/13632434.2014.943171.

McCray, C. R., & Beachum, F. D. (2014b). *School leadership in a diverse society: Helping schools prepare all students for success*. Charlotte, NC: Information Age Publishing.

McCray, C. R., & Beachum, F. D . (2011). School leaders and their understanding of social and cultural capital. In R. Bartee (Ed.) *Contemporary perspectives on capital in educational context*. Charlotte, NC: Information Age Publishing.

McCray, C. R., Beachum, F. D., & Yawn, C. R. (2012). Educational salvation: Integrating critical spirituality for educational leadership in urban schools. *Catholic Education: A Journal of Inquiry and Practice, 16*(1), 90–114.

Milner, H. R. (2006). But good intentions are not enough: Theoretical and philosophical relevance in teaching students of color. In J. Landsman & C. W. Lewis (Eds.), *White teachers/diverse classrooms: A guide to building inclusive schools, promoting high expectations, and eliminating racism* (pp. 79–90). Sterling, VA: Stylus.

Milner, H. R. (2010). *Start where you are but don't stay there: Understanding diversity, opportunity gaps, and teaching in today's classrooms*. Cambridge, MA: Harvard Education Press.

Moore, J. L., III, & Lewis, C. W. (2012). *African American students in urban schools: Critical Issues and solutions for achievement*. New York: Peter Lang.

Perry, T. (2003). Up from the parched earth: Toward a theory of African-American achievement. In T. Perry, C. Steel, & A. G. Hilliard (Eds.), *Young gifted and Black: Promoting high achievement among African-American students* (pp. 1–108). Boston: Beacon.

Prier, D. D. (2012). *Culturally relevant teaching: Hip-hop pedagogy in urban schools*. New York: Peter Lang.

Ryan, J. (2006). *Inclusive leadership*. San Francisco, CA: Jossey-Bass.

Strike, K. A., Haller, E. J., & Soltis, J. F. (1998). *The ethics of school administration* (2nd ed.). New York: Teachers College Press.

Tatum, B. D. (2007). *Can we talk about race? And other conversations in an era of school resegregation.* Boston, MA: Beacon Press.

Villegas, A. M., & Lucas, T. (2002). *Educating culturally responsive teachers: A coherent approach.* Albany, NY: State University of New York Press.

West, C. (2008). *Hope on a tightrope: Words and wisdom.* Carlsbad, CA: Hay House, Inc.

Young, I. M. (1990). *Justice and the politics of difference.* Princeton, NJ: Princeton University Press.

Chapter 7

Visionary Curriculum: A Journey, Not a Destination

Selma K. Bartholomew and Ingrid Lafalaise

INTRODUCTION

The sense of urgency to define a visionary curriculum for our nation's learners has never been more pressing than now in light of globalization, technology, and the reality of a stagnating economy. The National Center for Education Statistics notes that about one-third of the fourth graders and one-fifth of the eight graders cannot perform basic computations, and U.S. high school students for decades continue to fall behind international competitors.

Education has always been tied to opportunity; however, today the question on the goals of curriculum has led to a tsunami of reforms, which includes the implementation of Common Core Standards, charter versus public school debate, increased accountability, and reforms that tout outcomes-based results for learners with all reforms hinged on implementing a curriculum that will better prepare our learners and make them more competitive.

We are at the beginning of the twenty-first century, and within just the first two decades, we have seen revolutionary technological advances in communication. Despite all of these changes, our approach to education has stayed relatively the same. We still subscribe to the basic big four core courses: English, math, social studies, and science and still believe that learning takes place mostly in a *building* where we house students for just under seven hours per day.

This model has been the dominant approach to education since the industrial revolution. But, as the technology is changing at a rapid pace, we must also make changes to our approach to teaching and learning for students to be adequately prepared for this new millennium.

Historically, the decisions about a curriculum were made from central and district offices without much school involvement. Unfortunately, our schools

80   *Chapter 7*

seem to be unable to develop the capacity successfully to implement curriculum reforms and create meaningful change. Hargreaves (1998) notes that educational change is difficult because the "change is too broad and ambitious so that teachers have to work on too many fronts, or it is too limited and specific so that little change occurs at all" (p. 281).

The flood of changes often leaves our school leaders and teachers feeling overwhelmed and sadly not optimistic because they perceive these reforms as top-down and coming from politicians and external agents who are unaware of the "real" issues schools are facing.

This chapter on a visionary curriculum addresses the goals of a visionary curriculum that will move our children into the twenty-first century. The diagram in the following reminds us that a visionary curriculum is a process

Figure 7.1. **Finishing the Race**

and a journey, not a static destination. Before educators can reach a visionary curriculum, they must first articulate the fears that are within their learning culture, which are hurdles that may be holding them back from reaching a visionary curriculum.

The model also demonstrates that teachers and learners are in the race together toward a curriculum that innovates and integrates for the purpose of inspiring growth and change. The innovation for a visionary curriculum must place collaboration as a centerpiece.

WE ARE HERE: OVERCOMING THE FEARS

School reforms are short-lived, because the challenge of identifying and overcoming the fears and ingrained beliefs of the stakeholders is rarely addressed. Peter Senge (1990) writes that "ultimately, vision is intrinsic not relative. It is something you desire for its intrinsic value, not because of where it stands you relative to another. Relative vision may be appropriate in the interim, but they will rarely lead to greatness" (p. 149). To reach a visionary curriculum, educators should first provide attention to the fears, which are hurdles and obstacles that keep us from reaching a visionary curriculum.

During the unpacking of the fears and obstacles, educators will discover that teachers and instructional leaders have very different understandings and perceptions about *what is a curriculum*.

In addition, stakeholders often do not trust the innovation or have enough time to develop an understanding of the rationale for the innovation. Communication channels between stakeholders become stifled when limited time must be shared for professional development, administrative issues, testing coordination, student discipline, and the implementation of mandates.

DEFINING A CURRICULUM

One of the major setbacks to implementing a visionary curriculum within schools is the perception that the district is supposed to *hand or deliver* the curriculum to teachers and the school completed and ready for implementation. This hurdle is a challenge for instructional leaders and all stakeholders because of the limited knowledge and varied understanding among stakeholders about *what is a curriculum*.

To reach a visionary curriculum, we need a more thoughtful definition of a curriculum. A curriculum is a process that articulates what all students should know, understand, and be able to do within the following key components: *the hidden, the recommended, the written, the taught, the tested, the learned, the supported, and the null.*

Table 7.1. Fears and Hurdles Keeping Us from Visionary Curriculum

Leaders	Teachers	Students	Parents	Community
Uncertain about how to go about identifying or developing a visionary curriculum and how to develop teacher capacity to ensure effective lesson planning and delivery. Feeling overwhelmed with having to do so many teacher evaluations. Getting constant feedback from outside school due to state metrics and not having enough resources and time to address the feedback or make significant curriculum structures. Feeling powerless in moving ineffective teachers out of the classroom. Uncertainty about how to manage teacher development and monitor progress.	The belief that the district should "hand" a curriculum. Perceptions of student apathy and lack of student engagement is frustrating and overwhelming. "These" kids are too far behind grade level and need basic skills in reading and math. Fears of letting go of old lesson plans. The curriculum is the textbooks and the worksheets.	Feeling confined to a time structure that was designed for working parents, not necessarily students. School is boring and not motivating. Feeling unengaged and anxious about learning outcomes. Not sure if college is a choice and feelings of uncertainty. Limited ownership of learning outside of the classroom and school day.	Finding time and energy to build relationships with teachers and schools is difficult during workdays. Feeling ashamed when students are failing and uncertain about what to do with students to keep them motivated. What resources do they use to help students who may be failing. Fear that public schools are not working. Given changing family structures are teachers considering?	Fear and perceptions that public schools are not working. Creating meaningful job opportunities for members of the community is challenging. The public school vs. charter school debate creates a polarized discourse. Conflicting messages from the news and school about what is a curriculum. The new CCLS (Center for Computational Learning Center) is the curriculum?

Having a deeper understanding of all the components of a curriculum will allow teachers, parents, leaders, students, and community to better articulate in what areas what is working and what is not working and strategies for improvement. More important, it will facilitate the discussion that a visionary curriculum is a process not a product. For example, policy makers and educators devote a great deal of time and resources to the standards and textbooks and to the professional development to help deepen teachers' pedagogy.

However, little attention is provided to the hidden curriculum, the underlying values and beliefs of stakeholders, who are responsible for implementing a visionary curriculum within schools.

To implement a visionary curriculum that seeks to innovate and integrate, educators should consider the hidden curriculum and elements of resistance from all stakeholders. For example, students may resist an innovation if they don't believe that they don't have a strong sense of *self-efficacy* and don't expect to gain the levels that they are told they will achieve with a new curriculum or they may not value the stated outcomes. The hidden curriculum also speaks to how children and learning are celebrated within daily instruction.

Are teachers working *collaboratively* to send a message to children that they are supported by all members of the learning community? Are students encouraged to *collaborate* and question themselves, their peers, and their teachers? Are students anonymous unless they seek the attention of the teacher? All of these are important questions instructional leaders and teachers must consider when seeking to implement a visionary curriculum and changes in instructional practices.

COLLABORATION IS THE INNOVATION

Rogers (2003) defines an innovation as an idea, practice, or object that is perceived as new by an individual or other unit of adoption. Consider the innovation of kindergarten, which was not always a part of American education. In 1850 a German educator named Frederick Froebel conceptualized the innovative idea of a "child's garden" and a place for young children to play and learn.

Froebel and his ideas were shunned within Germany, and it took more than twenty years for the innovation of kindergarten to spread throughout Europe. By World War I, kindergartens were everywhere. Rogers (2003, p. 64) suggests that the innovation of kindergarten was able to be diffused within our nation because it fits with national values and to the larger politics.

Today our personal lives and businesses are experiencing rapid technology change based on the theory of pull. The Internet and so much of our

Table 7.2. Defining a Curriculum: What *All* Students Should Know, Understand, and Be Able to Do

Hidden Curriculum	Underlying beliefs and "modeled" practices which *silently scream* what teachers and leaders believe about how children learn, and their expectations for *all* learners (students and adults). • Learning culture • Student voice • Celebrations • Attention to college and career readiness
Recommended Curriculum	The recommended curriculum includes the state standards and benchmarks for student learning. • Standards • Benchmarks • State assessments
Written Curriculum	The written curriculum includes all the written products that support daily instruction for learners. • Textbooks and all supporting resources • District and school packing calendars, curriculum alignment documents, and scope and sequence documents • Lesson plans • Worksheets and graphic organizers
Taught Curriculum	The taught curriculum is the intersection of the content knowledge and pedagogical content knowledge of teachers. • Teachers' instructional delivery of the written curricula • Implementation of best practices on how to ensure high student engagement • Attention to core instructional strategies which includes the habits of minds within and across disciplines
Tested Curriculum	The tested curriculum: • Provides teachers with informal and formal assessments which serve as tools for re-teaching, challenging, and identifying new learning goals for *all* learners • Provides the evidence of student learning
Learned Curriculum	Student work is the artifact of teaching and demonstrates the intent of the learner. • Student motivation • Self-efficacy • Grade-level performance
Supported Curriculum	• Supplemental resources that support your core instructional program • After-school and enrichment curriculum • Technology and other learning tools that support *all* learners.
Null Curriculum	• Educators are unable to predict the future. Technology and the needs of society are constantly changing. • For example, thirty years ago we could not envision the importance of a course in statistics or Excel in preparing students for college and career readiness.

technology allow us and our businesses to easily access, attract, and achieve goals. The ability to pull desired knowledge, information, and resources means that industries are no longer solely based in the United States, and the boundaries of a business are no longer defined by a physical location. Pull has also changed core values where we can longer talk about collaboration—collaboration is necessary for survival. This decoupling of business from borders has also resulted in a multigenerational workforce, which includes millennials, baby boomers, and generation X, and also workers are from diverse cultures.

We know what innovation looks like and feels like in the context of the technology that impacts the quality of our day-to-day lives. However, in the context of the classroom we must ask what is not consistently happening in the classroom? What shifts and practices must be embraced and re-invented to create a spark for the learner and for teachers? To reach a visionary curriculum the innovation is *collaboration*.

A visionary curriculum must create the structures and purposeful opportunities for students to develop a comprehensive understanding of the skill sets of what it means to work collaboratively with neighbors and global citizens. Collaboration must become a vehicle to make new knowledge. The idea of collaboration is not new to educators, however the unfortunate reality is that it has not taken hold within schools and classrooms.

We know that learning is socially constructed, and yet that belief does not permeate all aspects of the curriculum:

> Every function in the child's cultural development appears twice: first on the social level and later, on the individual level; first, between people (interpsychological) and then inside the child (intra-psychological). This applies equally to voluntary attention, to logical memory and to the formation of concepts. All the higher functions originate as actual relationships between individuals (Vgotzy, 1978, p. 57).

The model below reflects the goals for collaboration for the learner. It demonstrates that the boundaries of the classroom must be open to allow for collaboration to take place within and beyond the traditional classroom walls.

To reach an innovative curriculum, the classroom and school building must become permeable and allow ideas to flow into and out of the learning environment through a process of diffusion. Rogers (2003) notes, "diffusion is a particular type of communication in which the message content that is exchanged is concerned with a new idea. The essence of the diffusion process is the information exchange through which one individual communicates a new idea to one or several others" (p. 15).

To reach a visionary curriculum, educators must create opportunities for students to collaborate with other students within the school and external to the school. The goals of collaboration rest on all domains of the curriculum

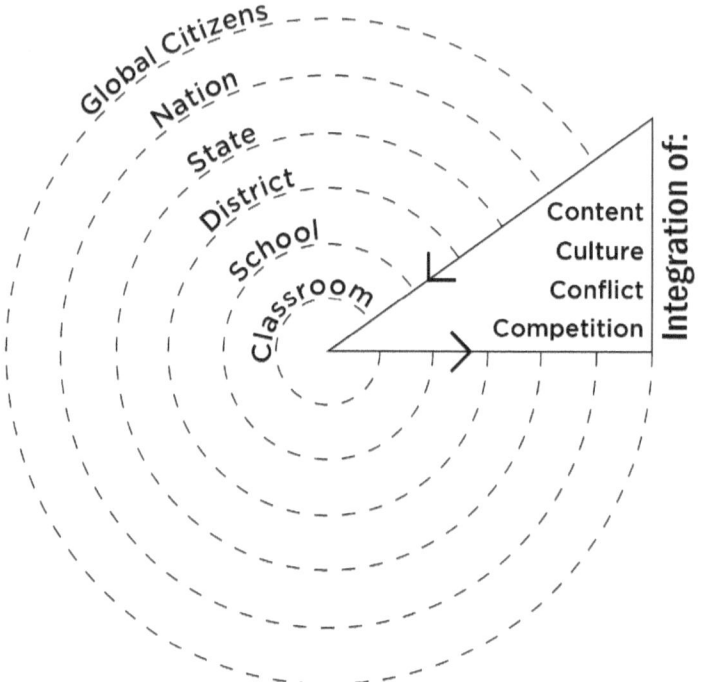

Figure 7.2. Multi-Pronged Levels of Creating a Student/Learner-Centered Classroom

as defined earlier, shifting from a teacher-centered classroom to a student/learner-centered classroom. When students collaborate to solve a problem, the possibilities are limitless. For example, in the film *Most Likely to Succeed*, we learn about visionary schools that have flipped the traditional school model. The goals of these schools are to reimagine education and provide students opportunities to innovate and create new ideas, integrate knowledge across content to solve problems, and think critically about situations presented before them. These schools are able to meet the demand of new thinking of the twenty-first century. Imagine if all schools are able to diverge from the constraints of the traditional school system and create opportunities for teaching and learning that are authentic and meet students' needs.

The key to a visionary curriculum is collaboration. This model of *collaboration* would not be complete without attention to *integration*. Consider that every year countless individuals make new year's resolutions to get fit and finally get the last ten pounds off. The usual start out includes going to the gym and getting a personal trainer.

However, if the strategies and actions are not integrated and become part of the daily ritual, the goals will not be met. In the context of education very little attention has been provided to integration. The traditional curriculum is fragmented, and to reach a new vision, educators must now learn about what it means to integrate and pull for new knowledge.

Educators must divorce themselves from the notion that significant learning can only take place in the classroom with the teacher at the helm. Children constantly receive stimuli from multiple sources. They must contextualize these experiences, reflect and make sense of all the information they receive.

Traditional curriculum models do not create opportunity for these experiences. They relegate students to a top-down model of knowledge construction in which students do not have an active role. Curriculum has been traditionally been designed as a sequence of content knowledge students are expected to master.

A visionary curriculum will revolutionize what educators will see as true demonstration of knowledge. Understanding is not the regurgitation of facts on a state exam, it is the ability for students to demonstrate repeatedly how one is able to take a set of skills and content and apply to a novel situation. A visionary curriculum builds in opportunities for integration and collaboration thus allowing for incorporation of information from multiple sources, and application of this information to new situations and solving to solve real-world problems.

The chart below highlights key areas that educators must consider to move our students to the twenty-first century. These include content integration, culture, conflict, and competition. Content integration breaks us away from teaching the big four courses in isolation, because in the real world it is integrated not compartmentalized, yet we continue to teach this way. To truly understand the problem you have to be able to examine the problem and problem-solving through multiple lenses.

For example, a ninth-grade culminating project can include students studying a local watershed and examine the history and pollution of the watershed. They will then design a solution to the pollution problem and present their project at a local community board meeting. A project of this caliber when further unpacked can infuse algebra, science, history, engineering, English, and technology. Students will learn the content as they work toward a solution to this culminating problem and real-world task.

They will also be able to pull beyond the walls of their classroom the research and experts needed to inform their discourse. The content does not have to be taught as individualized and separate units unto themselves. Most importantly, students will work to innovate a solution to a problem, collaborate with others to find a solution, and present ideas and research to a group. These are the skills that will have meaning in the twenty-first century. If we provide students the opportunity to further fine-tune these skills, then they will be better prepared for the necessities of the twenty-first-century world of work. A visionary curriculum centered on the innovation of collaboration and integration for the learner will provide the attention necessary for students to achieve and become independent and reflective learners.

A visionary curricula seeking to meet the needs of learners must attend to the following:

Table 7.3. Collaboration and Integration Model—Learner-Centered

Content Integration	Culture	Collaboration	Competition
Provide attention to:	Provide attention to:	Provide attention to:	Provide attention to:
• Integrating content to help students make sense of real-world applications • Exploring knowledge in various subject matters • Learning is transferred • Problem-solving across different subject matters • Real-world problems on a local level within the school, district, state, and nation • Problem-solving strategies and how they are utilized within subject • Interdisciplinary approaches to problem-solving	• Students reflecting on their classroom culture and having choice in ways to harness student voice • Understanding community culture and issues impacting their community • Understanding diverse cultures and how culture affects decision-making and solutions	• How students deal with conflict as they work with peers across all levels • How different cultures deal with conflict • Strategies for conflict resolution • How different generations deal with conflict	• The role of competition and students' beliefs about when and how they compete • Understanding the role of technology and how the rapidly changing technology impacts competition and outcomes • Defining self-efficacy and articulating goals that serve to motivate and keep on course

The challenges students are facing from social disorganization, which results in poverty, gun violence, unemployment, single-parent households, and other nontraditional family structures, demand that schools help children develop the emotional capacity to face these challenges. Schools cannot ignore the trauma children experience at home and in the broader community.

As a result of trauma they find it difficult to self-soothe, resolve conflict, and buy into the curriculum.

More important, children find it difficult to pay attention in class and display difficult behaviors for teachers to manage, which result in higher suspension rates and referrals to special education.

We can no longer ignore the need for a more balanced curriculum and instructional strategies that address character development of students. This cannot be a supplement to the curriculum; schools must address conflict within the schools and the broader society more purposefully and then integrate character development into the core curriculum.

COMPETITION

Often when designing curriculum, little consideration is given to the learners themselves. District administrators, school-level administrators, and teachers regularly design meaningful tasks with little input from students. Student voice is an integral part to students' buy-in of curriculum.

We often complain that students lack motivation; yet conclude that the motivation is only determined by an internal set of factors and remove our "shutting out of student voice" to this lack of motivation. Our students are not fully aware that they are no longer just competing on a local level for opportunities in education and career.

A visionary curriculum will provide opportunities for students to self-discover, thus increasing motivation. An increase in motivation will build student's self-efficacy, which means that efficacy refers a student's self-belief in completing a task. Schunk (1991) defines self-efficacy as "an individual's judgments of his or her capabilities to perform given actions" (p. 207); and Bandura (1986) defines it as "people's judgments of their capabilities to organize and execute courses of action required to attain designated types of performance" (p. 391).

One's belief in one's ability often plays a critical role in motivation and academic achievement. Students' beliefs about their capabilities are often more influential in terms of what they are capable of accomplishing than their actual capacity. This belief, therefore, is a great predictor of student behavior. When students are engaged in meaningful work that they participated in creating, their investment in the task will be magnified.

COLLABORATION FOR TEACHER

The act of teaching involves both the teacher and the learner. Yet we know that teaching lies within the control of teachers (Stigler & Hiebert, 1999).

Having a visionary written textbook or product for learners within the classroom environment is not enough to get improved outcomes for learners. For example, principals are constantly urged to buy more technology for teachers that includes white interactive boards. However, these have not served to innovate teaching, and the traditional talk and chalk are now replaced with static PowerPoint talk and click—yet student engagement or performance has not necessarily increased.

The road to an innovative curriculum requires a commitment to helping teachers and stakeholders understand that the process of developing and implementing a visionary curriculum *culminates* then grows roots for extension with the teacher and the student within the classroom.

To provide attention to collaboration as the innovation for the learner alone would be a deficient model. A visionary curriculum must also reach for collaboration among teachers and stakeholders within the school community.

A visionary curriculum must create a paradigm shift for educators from the historical mind-set of innovation occurring as a result of an inventor who works in a laboratory setting or for a business to develop a new technology. Chesbrough (2003) defines the concept of open innovations as a process that moves innovation beyond the boundaries of a particular innovation for business. As *open teacher innovators*, the purposeful work of designing and implementing well-developed lesson plans become central to the efforts of teaching.

During that planning process, the design of lesson is driven by the goal of making the classroom into a laboratory. The lesson plans should allow students greater choice and participation within the learning. The culminating written curriculum seeks to open up the classroom to student voice and to make learning the focus rather than teaching.

Teachers *talk about* collaboration with students and tell them that they need to collaborate to succeed; however, students are always experiencing the hidden curriculum within school that reveals the evidence of collaboration and true teamwork among teachers, leaders, and students. In spite of the need for collaboration in the work world, teaching remains isolated and the classroom, an island.

To implement a visionary written curriculum successfully, teachers need structured and consistent opportunities to collaborate with their peers and with others beyond the boundaries of the school building to exchange ideas. Collaboration is key to teachers becoming a cohesive team and moving beyond the boundaries of the traditional departmental structure which is preventing the diffusion of ideas.

Collaboration with professionals outside of the boundaries of school is also essential to the process of diffusion. Just as students are trapped in the traditional structures of the school day, teachers are also confined in the same

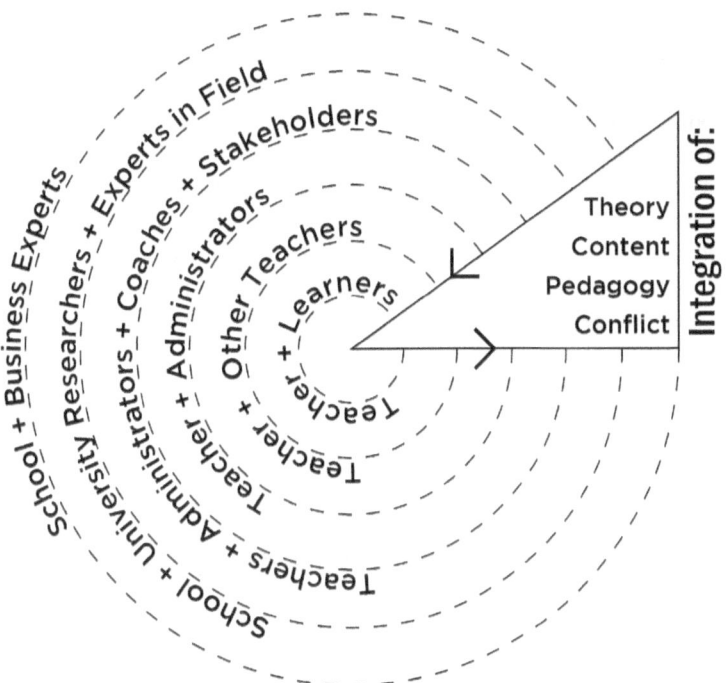

Figure 7.3. Moving from the macro to the micro

structures. Teachers need purposeful access to experts so that they can make better sense of the content and application of the content in the real-world settings. For example, teachers are often urged to provide students real-world examples of what they are learning.

However, the reality is that teachers do not have facilitated connections with members of the working and research communities to articulate some of the immediate and pressing problems in the field and how experts go about problem-solving.

Creating structures for collaboration is not enough; stakeholders also need to learn concretely about what well-developed collaboration looks like, feels like, and sounds like.

The model also provides attention to integration. Schools and districts have been giving attention to frameworks for teaching that focus on domains such as question and engaging learners; however they must reach for the big idea of integration. The reality is that a great lesson reflects the seamless integration of theory, content, pedagogy, and collaboration. The process of getting to a visionary curriculum should provide greater attention and a meaningful feedback on how well teachers *integrate*.

The education research has provided significant attention to the need to improve the content knowledge, the pedagogical content knowledge of teachers, and the beliefs about how children learn. Content knowledge addresses the depth and understanding of a teacher to make sense of the subject matter for learners. However, if we consider the example in the area of mathematics, knowing the math does not necessarily make you a great mathematics teacher.

One must also have within skill sets the pedagogical content knowledge to create a learning environment that engages learners and makes the content accessible to them. The diagram below demonstrates the connection between theory, content, pedagogy, and collaboration, which come together as a result of how well teachers are able to integrate what they know and understand what results in a highly effective taught curriculum.

Integration is evident when teachers are confidently able to explain and justify that what they are doing fits in the broader goals for learners and the

Table 7.3. Collaboration and Integration Model Teachers

Theory	Content	Pedagogy	Collaboration
• Theories and beliefs about how children learn • Theories and beliefs about adult learning • Theories and beliefs about parent and community	• Teachers seek to develop a deeper understanding of the content knowledge and how to make sense of content for learners • Planning and teaching provide consistent attention to what all students should know, understand, and be able to do • Content is relevant to what is happening today and makes connections to the past and future • Integrate technology, tools, and media that matter to learners	• Instructional strategies such as questioning, summarizing, and reflecting are integrated into planning and implementation of lesson • Differentiation of process, product, and assessment and to meet varied learning styles • Strategies demonstrated to check for student understanding • Assessments with ongoing feedback and opportunities to assess students working independently and with peers	• Teachers working together to develop and refine all domains of the curriculum and taking ownership of coauthoring content and pedagogy • Teachers learning and reflecting on how to work in teams • Teachers and all stakeholders learning how to deal with conflict that arise from collaboration

Visionary Curriculum 93

school community. The graph below shows the trajectory of integration of teaching and the relationship to the development of learners. As teachers are proficient at integrating the theory, content, pedagogy, and collaborating, the learner moves from consumer to becoming reflective.

The following are the three domains of curriculum readiness that teachers should be cognizant of as they work with student on different levels.

Proficiency: Teachers are consistently able to take full advantage of the features of all domains of the curriculum. They are skilled at including the available technology and resources to increase student engagement. The taught curriculum demonstrates consistent ability to utilize varied instructional strategies to make complex ideas more tangible and make connections to real world enabling students to reflect on problem, problem-solving, and their roles and responsibilities to society and community. Students are collaborators who naturally turn to each other to talk without prompting or dissonance. The classroom discourse and lesson focus on big ideas and making connections to real world for learners.

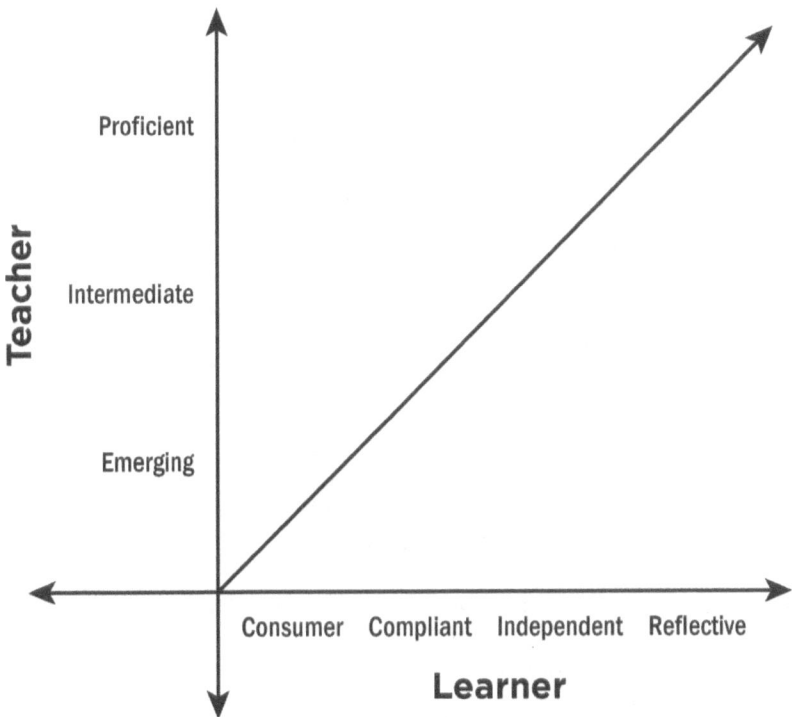

Figure 7.4. Relationship of Teacher and Learner

Intermediate: Teachers take ownership of creating learner-centered classrooms and ensure that collaboration structures are present within the learning culture. Teachers are able to implement the textbook but with some modifications around the diverse needs of learners.

Emergence: Teachers voice the "usefulness" and awareness of the curriculum but does not demonstrate a readiness to implement. Classroom culture and lessons are more teacher-led and student work reflect copying, worksheets and students as consumers. Students may be sitting structurally in groups; however there is no evidence of the goals of engendering collaboration. Lessons focus more on facts.

CONCLUSION

One has much to be considered when discussing the components of a visionary curriculum. Though we continue to tie student success to education, the fundamentals of education have not changed enough to catch up to the changes in technology and globalization of the twenty-first century. Students must be able to develop content through collaboration with others, and the integration of content and ideas that are not restricted to the traditional big four courses. A visionary curriculum shifts from the focus on student memorizing facts to making learning the focus of teaching.

To prepare students for success, we are called upon rethink the goals of curriculum. A visionary curriculum must provide students opportunities to engage in the skills that are valuable for success in the new century and must provide teachers/schools/school districts the ability to create these opportunities for students. We must find the time and space necessary to significantly prepare students for the demand of the new millennium. Visionary curriculums must meet the demands of preparing students for this shift of what it means to be successful. Then and only then will we be able to inspire our students, staff, and school community to rise to the occasion of successfully preparing the next generation of learners.

REFERENCES

Bandura, A. (1986). *Social foundation of thought and action: A social cognitive theory*. Englewood Cliffs, NJ: Prentice Hall.

Chesbrough, H. W. (2003). *Open innovation: The new imperative for creating and profiting from technology*. Boston: Harvard Business School Press.

Hargreaves, A. (1998). Pushing the boundaries of educational change. In A. Hargreaves, A. Lieberman, M. Fullan, & D. Hopkins (Eds.), *International handbook of educational change* (pp. 281–296). Dordrecht, Netherlands: Kluwer.

Rogers, E. M. (2003). *Diffusion of innovation* (5th ed.). New York: Simon and Schuster.

Schunk, D. H. (1991). Self-efficacy and academic motivation. *Educational Psychology, 26*, 207–231.

Senge, P. M. (1990). *The fifth discipline: The art and practice of the learning organization.* New York: Doubleday.

Stigler, J., & Hiebert, J. (1999). *The teaching gap: Best ideas form the world's teachers in improving education in the classroom.* New York: Simon and Schuster.

Vgotsky, L. S. (1978). *Mind in society: The development of higher psychological processes.* London: Harvard University Press.

Chapter 8

Putting Vision into Practice: Exploring Five Timeless Principles for Student Achievement

Jonathan W. Shute

Most teachers want to make a difference in the lives of children. Of course, this is noble, but the barrage of student problems related to mediocrity, entitlement, discipline, and downright disrespect, or after hours spent planning effective lessons and mastering skills, or during the mounting pressure for high test scores, this desire to "make a difference" alone does not sustain teachers year after year.

Alarmingly, research shows only one in fourteen teachers engage students in a stimulating classroom environment (Haberman, 2011). Thus, many students claim that school is boring and nonengaging (Sousa, 2011; Yazzie-Mintz, 2009). And since 1978, the number of students, who feel that attending school is rewarding and meaningful, has seen a consistent, steady, disastrous decline ("The Condition of Education 2002," p. 72).

No wonder unacceptably high truancy (both cutting school and missing certain classes) and dropout rates continue to plague our schools (Chesney-Lind, 2007; Roderick et al., 1997; Shute & Cooper, 2014). Indeed, in view of these enormous problems, students and parents are crying out for better schools, better teachers, and better learning environments. Collectively, our goals for student achievement through engaging lessons and active learning are clearly not being met.

This chapter explores five timeless and truly visionary principles which, if understood and put into practice, will make a profound difference in student learning. These include (1) the power of example, (2) the power of teaching to learn, (3) the power of teacher beliefs/metaphors, (4) the power of mastering skills, and (5) the power of student engagement through active learning.

HOW VISIONARY TEACHERS CAN TEACH BY EXAMPLE

Most people believe children—and people in general—learn best by example. Research substantiates this idea, as Albert Bandura (1997), a leading expert in social learning theory, has stated: "Fortunately, most human behavior is learned observationally through modeling: from observing others one forms an idea of how new behaviors are performed, and on later occasions this coded information serves as a guide" (p. 22).

When applying these ideas of "teacher example" and "teacher modeling" in education, these concepts are usually grouped with other teaching strategies contrived to influence student behavior and achievement. For example, teachers write a math equation on the board and give examples on how to solve it. Teachers model the way they want students to follow classroom procedures and use equipment in chemistry and biology classes.

When the example or model is taught carefully, it will have a positive effect on learning: for example, classroom procedures are more efficiently followed; math problems are more easily solved; and equipment in chemistry will less likely be used improperly. The twist in this common understanding of "example" and "modeling" in the classroom is that in reality, although most teachers don't realize it, nor do they want to believe it, they are modeling behavior *all of the time*.

And since "teacher modeling" and "teacher examples" are going on all of the time, students are learning from teachers' example modeled behavior *all of the time*. Usually, this deep learning is occurring without the conscious design of the teacher or the conscious awareness of the student.

According to Smith (1997), this powerful type of learning is sometimes referred to as "incidental" learning. We can easily see this idea at work in children. When a baby is young, no conscious effort is made to teach the child the language of her parents. The parents simply speak in their language to the child, and the child soon grows up speaking that language.

Whether the language is English, Spanish, Mandarin, Hebrew, or Arabic, it is incidentally learned by the child as a by-product without direct teaching, techniques, or strategies. "Learning about language is not the primary aim, but rather the by-product of some other activity" (p. 7). The parents simply spoke to the child about other things, and the child soon learned the language "incidentally."

A vast amount of other knowledge is learned, incidentally, by children; and research shows that children will imitate the behaviors of a model, whether it is a live person, a person on film, or even a cartoon character (Bandura, 1997). The behaviors being incidentally modeled to our children in movies, music, TV, and video games are being powerfully taught (and deeply learned), including violence, immorality, disrespect, and self-gratification.

In other words, the behaviors being powerfully taught can, of course, be equally good or bad. François Duc De La Rochefoucauld, a seventeenth-century French writer and moralist, said,

> Nothing is more contagious than an example, and no man does any exceeding good or exceeding ill but it spawns new deeds of the same kind. The good we imitate through emulation, the ill through the malignity of our nature, which shame keeps locked up, but example sets free. (Values.com, n.d.)

And visionary teachers understand and make use of this powerful principle of teaching and learning.

The power behind this principle speaks to the very identity of the learner—how they view themselves. This "identification is a psychological process whereby a person internalizes traits, attitudes, and behavioral patterns of another person whom one consciously or subconsciously wishes to emulate" (Beck, n.d.). Psychiatrist Carl Jung stressed that one of the oldest psychic attributes is the "unconscious education," taught through example, and "in the last analysis, all education rests on this fundamental fact of psychic identity, and in all cases the deciding factor is this seemingly automatic contagion through example" (cited in Beck, n.d.).

What a student learns from the teacher goes way beyond school content. That which is being modeled by the teacher is who they really are, at the very core, and what they stand for, their attitudes and beliefs. What a teacher is as a person is what he or she passes on to the student, mostly "incidentally."

In a classroom, this visionary idea is applied with every action and behavior the teacher does. This means, of course, that every reading and writing teacher should be a reader and a writer. When the school has as follows:

> A Drop Everything and Read (Sustained Silent Reading) time for your students, what are you doing? Are you grading papers, talking, or scolding students? If so, the message sent is that reading is important to students, but not to you. Pick up a book and read too. (Miller, n.d., p. 22)

This thus means that every history teacher should be a historian, and every biology teacher should be a biologist.

A visionary teacher loves learning; and so understandably, also the frustration common to most teachers is the lack of motivation that kids have toward learning. Many students react painfully to assignments and seem bored at almost everything that goes on in the classroom. A teacher may say over and over again that reading is important, but if the teacher doesn't read, if the student never sees the teacher reading for fun or for learning, then telling the child that reading is important is shallow talk.

In the *Read Aloud Handbook*, Jim Trelease (1982) states, "It's almost impossible to catch a cold from someone who doesn't have one. And it's almost impossible for a child to catch the love of reading from a teacher who doesn't have it" (cited in Miller, n.d.). If a child never sees the teacher reading, the message taught is that reading is *not important*, regardless of the words that are said.

"A student may not learn history in our history class, but he may learn that his teacher thinks history is interesting" (Zull, 2002, p. 20). Visionary teachers are thus on a quest for learning, and their students know it.

Great patriots and heroes throughout the ages are revered, honored, and more often than not, followed into death because they lived for their greatness. They did not sit behind a desk, teach one thing, and do another. As teachers, we can *live* what we teach. We can be historians, biologists, writers, and especially, lifelong learners, which, of course, is what we want all of our students to be.

VISIONARY TEACHERS UTILIZE TEACHING TO LEARN—*DOCEMUR DOCENDO*

Teaching to learn is a powerful principle to learn and master for visionary teachers who strive for excellence. Unfortunately, this principle is rarely consciously practiced as an effective strategy. Keep in mind that teaching to learn is not the same thing as student presentations or peer tutoring. These activities are transmitting-knowledge strategies. Because of the current value of knowledge as a thing to possess, our school system focuses on knowledge itself, not the *process* of learning it. Visionary teachers dethrone this erroneous view of knowledge by focusing on personalizing and making meaning of knowledge, which is the basis of teaching-to-learn principle.

Roman philosopher Seneca said, "While we teach, we learn" (cited in Paul & Elder, 2013). For thousands of years scholars have known that the best way to learn concepts is to explain them to someone (Paul & Elder, 2013). In the 1600s, John Comenius, a teacher in Moravia, described his philosophy in the following words taken from the *Didactica Magna*:

> The saying "he who teaches others, teaches himself," is very true, not only because constant repetition impresses a fact indelibly on the mind, but because the process of teaching in itself gives a deeper insight into the subject taught. If a student wished to make progress, he should arrange to give lessons daily in the subjects he was studying, even if he had to hire his pupils. (Shute, 1989, p. 43)

This time-honored method of *teaching to learn* has been recognized for at least 400 years, and is so important that students should hire someone to act as a student while you teach them the content you want to learn.

In the late 1700s, Andrew Bell, an Anglican cleric, who was head of an orphanage in India, developed teaching to learn, based on ancient Hindu educational practices, to allow the children to teach in order for them to learn. As Bell said, "The teacher profits far more by teaching than the scholar does by learning is a maxim of antiquity, which all experience confirms—*Docemur docendo*—he who teaches learns" (cited in Shute, 1989, p. 28).

Learning is tremendously enriched when visionary teachers use this principle. A study reported that significant gains were made by students who were told to study content material because they would be teaching it to their peers over students who were told to study content material in order to take a test (Nestojko, Bui, Kornell, & Bjork, 2014). Interestingly, even though the students did not actually teach the material, expecting to teach it produced gains in test scores. As Nestojko et al. (2014) explain,

> multiple measures of participants' responses converged to support the claim that expecting to teach promotes learning in ways that expecting a test does not . . . these findings suggest that participants processed information differently, and more effectively, when they expected to teach than when they expected to take a test. (p. 1043)

To teach, a teacher-student is forced to think about the material in one degree or another, for the purpose of internalizing it. The teacher must come to capture the knowledge, understand it, and shape it in somewhat new ways, according to his or her understanding. By doing this, he or she gains deeper, more meaningful insights into the subject.

Nestojko et al. (2014) conclude that students who expect to teach take on the mind-set of a teacher and use effective strategies many teachers use to teach. Examples are "organizing and weighing the importance of different concepts in the to-be-taught material, focusing on main points, and thinking about how information fits together" (Nestojko et al., 2014, p. 1046).

In other words, teaching to learn is more than simply a rote repetition of what one has been taught. Through the process of teaching something, the students really comes to internalize the material into their own way of thinking through a process of personalization—the process of deciding what meanings the material holds for them personally.

The students don't consciously set out to do this; but in the process of preparing to teach the ideas or concepts, it happens automatically (Shute, 1989). The students develop an expanded understanding of the material that they would never have achieved had they not been given the opportunity to teach.

This idea of *teaching by learning* requires a massive shift in the teaching paradigm and, in order to be effective, takes great planning. Some teachers may claim that this powerful principle would take too much time away from preparing the students for tests ever-looming overhead. Consider a 1983 study which revealed that students,

> who studied material thinking they would be required to teach it to others, even though they did not, scored significantly higher on tests than students who did not anticipate teaching. The research also showed that students who prepared to teach and then actually taught, significantly outscored those students who only prepared to teach. (Shute, 1989, p. 30)

In other words, the research by Nestojko et al. showed that students who expected to teach and didn't teach scored higher on tests than the students who studied expecting to take a test. Furthermore, students who studied material and actually taught it scored higher on tests than students who studied the material to teach but didn't actually teach it. This timeless, visionary principle of teaching and learning, effectively employed, is able to raise test scores.

This visionary teaching idea has more recently been put into practice by Dr. Jean-Pol Martin, who has done extensive research on teaching by learning. Martin discovered numerous positive benefits with this teaching principle. He explains that students' motivation and participation dramatically increased while students' reticence decreased. In addition, "a feeling of solidarity developed" and the division between teacher as the authority and students as a passive audience "evaporated" (Skinner, 2009, p. 22).

Visionary teachers will imagine the achievement gains of students in a classroom which prepared them to teach concepts, not only to their peers but also, specifically, for their teacher. Perhaps maximum learning would occur as Shute found:

> There is power inherent in the act of the taught verbalizing his knowledge for his teacher. Not only is the students' knowledge shaped more precisely through the act of teaching it, the teachers learn, in a unique way, how effective their own teaching has been. (1989, p. 31)

Other magical outcomes occur for students. First, obviously, the student's confidence grows by leaps and bounds. The student gains a sense of pride in that he or she is the one who knows the most; and that he or she, for this short time, is the most important person in the room. Second, when the students become the teacher, they begin to realize that teaching is no easy task. They come to appreciate more the efforts of those who attempt to teach them.

A word of caution for visionary teachers who attempt to implement *Docemur docendo*—teaching to learn. Like most things of value, this principle takes effort to implement effectively; and we may not necessarily see immediate earth-shaking evidences of the benefits. In addition, students may not seem especially grateful for the opportunity to teach, especially after years of being spoon-fed information. The attitudes and growth that occur are deep and personal.

They are not measurable or even sometimes discernible; but this doesn't mean that they don't exist. Most teachers instinctively know that they learn their content simply because they study and learn it so that they can teach it. Once the powerful nature of the *Docemur docendo* principle of teaching and learning is understood, visionary teachers will find many ways to encourage its use.

VISIONARY TEACHERS MASTER SKILLS

When smartphones came out, many resisted. Finally, many kids got me one and showed me a thing or two about it, but everything seemed too complicated. One day my daughter sent me a text message while I was in a meeting. I saw the text and answered her during the meeting. *Wow.* Suddenly, like the snowball effect, the benefits of the smartphone flashed through my mind: I could check e-mails, use the calculator, and set the morning alarm.

Eventually, I discovered Facebook, and I could video chat with my granddaughter every day! The point is that as I became skilled at using more features, the more magical the smartphone became to me, not because the phone changed, but because I learned new skills. My vision of what a smartphone could do expanded as I learned the mechanics of how to use it.

The same concept is true with visionary leadership for teachers. As we learn new research-based effective skills and become masters at using them, our vision of what is possible in the classroom expands; not because the classroom changes, or because the students change. Our vision expands because we mastered new skills.

Eventually, after much experience and hard work, we begin to see that a classroom in which every single student loves learning and achieves his or her highest potential is possible and achievable. Our vision expands proportionately to our mastery of research-based skills. In other words, "we must learn the mechanics before the magic" (Arends, 2015, p. 304).

However, teachers can only be as visionary (magical) as their vision allows, and their vision is only held in check by their individual skills and situations. Arends, in *Learning to Teach*, explains this with an example from the National Football League (NFL). Superstar NFL quarterbacks can read every defense and, without thinking, respond automatically with skill, accuracy, and self-discipline even in the face of a safety blitz. Novice quarterbacks can't do this very well (p. 304).

The field hasn't changed; the rules haven't changed; and the defense still has only eleven players. The only difference is a mastery of skills. In fact, the coach's vision of possibilities during game-changing situations is only limited by quarterback's skills. So it is in every profession; there are superstars and not-superstars—and the difference is the mastery of skills.

Suppose we are strolling along the beach. Up ahead we notice a large dark shape being rolled around by the waves. "What is it?" we wonder. As we get closer, we see a big, gnarly piece of driftwood. Some people may only see a piece of driftwood. However, a master wood-carver would see much more: a strong octopus, a vicious swordfish, and an intricate double-hulled canoe. Depending on this wood-carver's skills, that lonely piece of driftwood could be anything. Hence, without mastery of wood-carving skills we only see driftwood.

In *Teach Like a Champion: 62 Techniques that Put Students on the Path to College*, Lemov (2015) explains that teachers are artisans "whose task is to study a set of tools and unlock the secrets of their use" (p. 1). Their vision of possibilities expands as their skills improve:

> We learn to strike a chisel with a mallet and refine the skill with time, learning at what angle to strike the chisel and how tightly to hold it. Someday, perhaps years later, observers may assess the philosophy expressed by what you create, but far more important than any theory is your proficiency with the lowly chisel. . . . A chisel appears mundane, but the more you understand it, the more it guides you to see what is possible. Rounding a contour with unexpected smoothness, the chisel causes you to realize, suddenly, that we could bring subtlety to facial expression, more tension to the muscles of the figure you are sculpting, and this changes your vision for it. Mastery of tools does not just allow creation; it informs it. (Doug, 2015, pp. 1–2)

Visionary teachers must know that "there is a tool box for closing achievement gaps, so it turns out. The contents have been forged by ten thousand teachers working quietly and usually without recognition at the end of cracked-linoleum hallways" (p. 3). Imagine a classroom where a teacher struggles. The students are unruly, disorganized, and disrespectful. The teacher has become negative, disheartened, and on the verge of changing careers. While in the same school, across the hall, another teacher's class is thriving.

The students are engaged and active participants in their learning. Did the first teacher just happen to get the "bad" kids, and the second teacher, luckily, just get the "good" kids. Many nonvisionary teachers may disagree, but the answer is, No! The second teacher has a vision of what her classroom should be—a vision driven by knowledge of effective teaching practices and a mastery of proven skills.

As teachers, our job is to learn and develop skills similar to a surgeon, an author, and an artist. Our vision will expand with diligent study, purposeful practice, and focused effort to master skills.

VISIONARY TEACHERS DEVELOP CORRECT METAPHORS

Metaphors have a commanding control on a teacher's behavior in the classroom. One reason our visions of the classroom don't change is because our beliefs/metaphors of teaching and learning are faulty. Research has shown that regardless of the number of teacher trainings attended, only one in fourteen teachers engage students in a stimulating classroom environment (Haberman, 2011). This catastrophe is related to the power of teachers' beliefs, which can be described as "deeply held commitments that they [teachers] act upon . . . the deep-seated ideas that define a person as a human being with a heart and soul as well as a mind" (p. 1). Most of us need a metaphor makeover. And, adjusting their beliefs and metaphors is what visionary teachers do.

Teacher beliefs begin at a young age. Research by Murphy, Delli, and Edwards (2004) suggests that teacher beliefs about teaching begin as early as second grade (cited in Arends, 2015, p. 34). Imagine the damage done if our metaphors are inappropriate. As Smith contends, "sometimes metaphors distort our understanding; they make us perceive and think in ways that are inappropriate. And the fact that they do so may not even be suspected. The most misleading metaphors are those that we do not think are metaphors at all" (pp. 93–94). Adjusting metaphors requires a colossal effort, especially since the reality of our metaphors goes unnoticed to us.

Since we are largely oblivious to the metaphors that drive us, and since they begin forming early in life, Haberman suggests that direct teaching of correct beliefs or metaphors "has proven elusive if not impossible" (2011, p. 6). However, Yero (2010) contends, acquiring new metaphors, while extremely difficult, is possible, and actually "can be liberating" (2010, p. 97). The important point to remember is that metaphors are not to be treated as trivial whims.

These beliefs affect all aspects of teaching, including achievement, expectations, diversity, and student relationships. Belief systems are the metaphors inside us that we need to make sense of the situations we find ourselves in. A metaphor is not something we carry around—and discard at any time. Postman (1995) explains that "a metaphor is not an ornament. It is an organ of perception. Through metaphors, we see the world as one thing or another" (p. 174). Teachers carry with them deep-seated metaphors that propel their actions each day.

What are teaching and learning metaphors? Postman (1995) describes some metaphors relating to the classroom. He asks,

> is the human mind a dark cavern (needing illumination)? A muscle (needing exercise)? A vessel (needing filling)? A lump of clay (needing shaping)?

A garden (needing cultivation)? . . . or a computer that processes data? And what of students? Are they patients to be cared for? Troops to be disciplined? Sons and daughters to be nurtured? Personnel to be trained? Resources to be developed? (1995, p. 174)

Think of it, the metaphors we carry around will determine our behaviors and actions in the classroom. "Educational researchers have consistently concluded that the metaphors teachers use to describe their work significantly influence their actions" (Yero, 2010, p. 52). In short, behind every teacher action and decision is a root metaphor (Bullogh, 2015). If the metaphors we live by are faulty, our actions in the classroom will not only hinder student achievement but also squash it.

The dominant faulty metaphor in education is the factory metaphor. This metaphor sees students as bottles entering the factory in batches (grade levels). Imagine the bottles (students) progressing along a conveyor belt as well-meaning, hardworking employees (teachers) pour in water to fill up the bottle (small bits and pieces of knowledge, a little here, a little there, until eventually, hopefully after twelve years, our children are full of knowledge), and we put a cap (graduation) on their head and proudly proclaim them ready to contribute to society (Shute & Cooper, 2014).

Traditional education sees a well-meaning teacher in front of the class "transmitting knowledge" to students, and students sitting at their desks absorbing as much of this information as they can. The teacher is the "dispenser" of knowledge, with different strategies on how to dispense it (Bullogh, 2015; Postman, 1995; Smith, 1988; Yero, 2010).

Another faulty metaphor in education sees the brain as a computer, an information-processing device (Postman, 1995; Smith, 1988; Yero, 2010). Of course, a computer is perfect for what it does—storing enormous amounts of information and data, and then recalling those data instantly. We spend countless hours and unimaginable amounts of money forcing our students' brains to do the same. In this metaphor we see a teacher who has the knowledge "inputting" it into the student's brain using one technique or another.

The student is required to "store" the data and retrieve them whenever called upon, whether in a discussion or on a test. The teacher becomes a technician, inputting information into the child's "computer," who then should be able to recall the data instantly. Learning, then, is all about data entry; and teaching, then, is all about techniques and strategies to achieve the highest test results, not about meaningful, deep learning (Shute & Cooper, 2014). Tragically, schools, teachers, and students are measured by this faulty metaphor.

To understand why this is an incorrect metaphor, we must grasp the *differences* between the mind and a computer. The human mind can do things the computer cannot do—and never be able to do. A human mind can think, imagine, weigh, ponder, grapple, wonder, judge, and make personal meaning. The mind, thankfully, has the power to consider things, think about life with all its ironies and paradoxes, with all its perplexities and problems, and from these search for meaning (Shute & Cooper, 2014).

With these metaphors propelling us, our goal is to discover the methods, strategies, and programs that help *input or transmit* knowledge efficiently. The end goal is the input of knowledge, *not* pondering, inquiring, making connections, weighing, and wondering—the hard work it takes to really learn. In essence, the techniques and strategies become the focus, diverting from the construction of a framework that leads to meaningful learning, creativity, and intelligence. Until the metaphor changes, the end goal will be the same—recall information on tests.

Many better metaphors of learning and teaching exist, which portray the engaged nature of teaching and learning, especially with regard to exploring, making connections, and action. One of these is to consider teaching and learning a voyage of exploration on a double-hulled canoe (Teaiwa, 2011). Long before Europeans discovered the Pacific Ocean, the seafaring people of Oceania had subsisted, survived, and explored its wide expanses on double-hulled canoes. Imagine the majesty of the scene:

> The canoe is readied. The crew help load crates of fruits and vegetables, water, rope, materials—tools needed for a successful voyage. In the classroom teachers and students work together, preparing for the voyage of learning.

Family members stand together on the beach and stare off into the horizon—perhaps noticing the storms off in the distance—with the gnawing feeling of uncertainty in what lies ahead for their sons. Would the voyage prepare them, uplift them, give them confidence to face the world? Or would they return broken, discouraged, and apathetic? At home, parents reflect on the upcoming days, months, and years their children will spend in the classroom. Will the school year prepare them for a changing future, or return them home broken and apathetic?

The crew performs individual, assigned tasks that are of vital importance to the success of the voyage. These explorers are mutually committed, cooperating, and communicating as they prepare to sail away from their familiar home out into the open sea. They gather around the captain eagerly awaiting his words. He has completed many voyages, unceasingly studying, learning, and preparing. He understands the sacred trust placed in him by the crew, their families, and the village.

Their very lives are at stake. This voyage is a matter of life and death. Believing this, he has become the expert in surviving and thriving using the stars and constellations, the currents and waves, the clouds, sky, and wind. In the classroom, the teacher is this visionary leader, committed to be a lifelong learner, always adjusting his or her practice to the latest proven research.

These students and their captain are living an explorer's dream, driven to learn, expand the horizons of their own minds, and break the limits of the shore. In the classroom, do our students and teachers consider themselves driven to learn, expand the horizons of their own minds? Or are their minds limited with doubt and boredom? Are we living an explorer's dream in the seas of our classrooms? Do our students work together unafraid of grappling with the content, wrestling with the wind, confronting the currents? Or, are we aimlessly adrift on meaningless curriculum and damaging pedagogy?

Imagine the thrill as this band of explorers launch into the sea. Will our classrooms ever feel this thrill? If our students are not an engaged and active part of their educational voyage, how can they explore the majesty and wide expanses and wonders of life?

VISIONARY TEACHERS ENGAGE STUDENTS THROUGH ACTIVE LEARNING

The term "student engagement" is commonly used in education today—but also misinterpreted. Visionary teachers know that two specific components must be present for students to be engaged: first, the level of commitment students have toward learning; and second, the depth of connections students make with their learning (Schlechty, 2011). Teachers have the power to make lessons more engaging, but doing so does not happen by chance. Lessons must be purposefully designed to increase the level of commitment that students have toward learning and the depth of connections students make with their education.

Visionary teachers foster student engagement through active learning that occurs when "the mind is actively engaged" (Schlechty, 2011, p. 17). Students report feeling more engaged when they are active participants and/or work and learn with their peers. Yet, the instructional models most often used are those least engaging in which students often do not play an active role, for example, continual teacher lectures (Yazzie-Mintz, 2010).

The inescapable fact about the brain is that, biologically, it is built perfectly for optimum learning through being active. Our brains "sense the environment, add up (or integrate) what they sense, and generate appropriate movements (actions): Sense—Integrate—Act" (Zull, 2002, p. 15). The sensory signals come at us all of the time. And, our brains are doing something with these signals all of the time. Everything about the brain is active—from blood flow to stimuli zapping across synapses. Visionary teachers will not stifle their students' naturally active brains.

The brain has about 100 billion neuronal networks with an estimated 10,000 connections per neuron. "There are ten to a hundred times more connections in our brain than there are cells in our body.... There is a neuronal network in our brain for everything we know" (Zull, 2002, pp. 97–98). The miracle is that any neuronal network in the brain can connect with any other network if the connection is a useful one (Zull, 2002, p. 100).

Obviously, making useful connections is important for learning, and our brains are designed and capable of making those connections. In addition, neuroscience also tells us that novelty, creativity, attention, emotion, risk-taking, and making mistakes are other imperative aspects of meaningful learning (Jensen, 2008; Sousa, 2011; Zull, 2002). Science of the brain tells us how the brain works but it cannot tell us how to teach. However, if visionary teachers understand how the brain works, they will figure out how to effectively teach.

Active learning—the learning which students desire—requires students to examine, question, relate, and use these billions of neurons to make connections with, and sense, the content through interaction with the teacher and peers rather than simply trying to absorb information transmitted to them (Weimer, 2013, p. 63). "People learn by confronting intriguing, beautiful, or important problems, authentic tasks that will challenge them to grapple with ideas, rethink their assumptions, and examine their mental models of reality" (Bain, 2004, p. 18).

Visionary teachers guide students through the active, deep learning that propels them to think, feel, and act differently as a result of what they learn (Bain, 2004). All too often classes are concentrated around a teacher's ideas, interests, connections, and applications. Teachers must switch the center of attention off themselves because only when students are grappling with concepts, can they really grab ahold of them. Teachers must be "focused on what the students are doing, instead of what they themselves are doing" (Weimer, 2013, p. 62). This change of focus is the catalyst for active learning.

CONCLUSION

Students are rational decision-makers, capable of understanding the difference between good and bad teaching, and meaningful and unmeaningful lessons. Many students are neither engaged in learning nor do they appear interested in becoming engaged in the current way education is delivered to them. They have become alienated and disengaged from school and class (Shute & Cooper, 2014). Over the decades, what students have been trying to tell us is they are not engaged or fulfilled with meaningful learning.

Visionary teachers will not only break this cycle of alienation and disengagement, but elevate learning to its rightful place among the most fulfilling, thrilling, and important activities in which to engage. Research show that "the most important factor affecting student learning is the teacher . . . more can be done to improve education by improving the effectiveness of teachers than by any other single factor" (cited in Marzano, 2003, p. 1).

Visionary teachers matter! Explore and make personalized meaning of how learning is best achieved by learners, thereby making learning engaging and fulfilling. If teachers do not grapple with and individualize learning about learning, our learning environments will continue to deteriorate. As much as the teacher is "determined to prepare [their] students for deep learning, as their teacher, [we] must prepare [ourselves] for deep learning about both teaching and learning" (Teaiwa, 2011, p. 214). Albert Einstein is quoted as saying, "We cannot solve our problems with the same thinking we used when we created them." We have a problem in education today that visionary teachers can solve with these timeless, proven principles.

REFERENCES

Albert Einstein. http://www.brainyquote.com/quotes/quotes/a/alberteins121993.html

Arends, R. I. (2015). *Learning to teach* (10th ed.). New York: McGraw-Hill Education.

Bain, K. (2004). *What the best college teachers do.* Cambridge, MA: Harvard University Press.

Bandura, A. (1997). *Self-efficacy: The exercise of control.* New York, NY: W. H. Freeman.

Beck, S. (n.d.) *Teaching by example.* Retrieved from http://www.san.beck.org/Teaching-by-Example.html

Bullogh, R. V., Jr. (2015). Methods for studying beliefs: Teacher writing, scenarios, and metaphor analysis. In H. Fives & M. G. Gill (Eds.), *International handbook of research on teachers' beliefs* (pp. 150–169). New York: Routledge.

CAST. (2011). *Universal design for learning guidelines version 2.0.* Wakefield, MA.

Chesney-Lind, M., et al. (2004, February). *Arrest trends, gang involvement, and truancy in Hawaii: An interim report to the twenty-second Hawaii state legislature.* Center for Youth Research, Social Science Research Institute, University of Hawaii at Manoa.

The Condition of Education (2002). National Center for Education Statistics. Page 72. Retrieved from http://nces.ed.gov/pubsearch/pubsinfo.asp?pubid=2002025

Guare, R., & Cooper, B. S. (2003). *Truancy revisited: Students as school consumers.* Lanham, MD: Scarecrow Press.

Haberman, M. (2011). *The beliefs and behaviors of star teachers.* Teachers.Net Gazette, August 2011.

Jensen, E. (2008). *Brain-based learning: The new paradigm of teaching.* Thousand Oaks, CA: Corwin Press.

Lemov, D. (2015). *Teach like a champion 2.0: 62 techniques that put students on the path to college.* The Condition of Education 2002. National Center for

Education Statistics. Page 72. Retrieved from http://nces.ed.gov/pubsearch/pubsinfo.asp?pubid=2002025 San Francisco, CA: Jossey-Bass.

Marzano, R., Marzano, J., & Pickering, D. (2003). *Classroom management that works: Research-based strategies for every teacher.* Alexandria, VA: Association for Supervision and Curriculum Development.

McCray, C. R., & Beachum, F. D., (2014a). Countering plutocracies: Increasing autonomy and accountability through culturally relevant leadership. *The Journal of School Leadership and Management.* doi: 10.1080/13632434.2014.943171.

McCray, C. R., & Beachum, F. D., (2014b). *School leadership in a diverse society: Helping schools prepare all students for success.* Charlotte, NC: Information Age Publishing.

McCray, C. R., Beachum, F. D., & Yawn, C. R. (2012). Educational salvation: Integrating critical spirituality for educational leadership in urban schools. *Catholic Education: A Journal of Inquiry and Practice, 16*(1), 90–114.

Miller, C. P. (n.d.). *Teaching reading by example.* Education World. Retrieved from http://www.educationworld.com/a_curr/columnists/miller/miller003.shtml

Nestojko, J. F., Bui, D. C., Kornell, N., & Bjork, D. L. (2014). Expecting to teach enhances learning and organization of knowledge in free recall of text passages. *Memory & Cognition, 42* (October 2014), 1038–1048. doi: 10.3758/s13421–014–0416-z. Retrieved from http://psych.wustl.edu/memory/nestojko/NestojkoBuiKornellBjork(2014).pdf

O'Keeffe, D. (1993). *Truancy in English secondary schools: A report prepared for the DFE.* London: HMSO.

Paul, R. & Elder, L. (2013). Critical Thinking: Tool for taking charge of your professional and personal life. Upper Saddle River, New Jersey: Pearson.

Postman, N. (1995). *The end of education: Redefining the value of school.* New York: Alfred A. Knopf, Inc.

Roderick, M., Arney, M., DaCosta, K., Steiger, C., Stone, S., Villarreal-Sosa, L., & Waxman, E. (1997, July). *Habits hard to break: A new look at truancy in Chicago's public high schools.* University of Chicago. Retrieved from http://ccsr.uchicago.edu/sites/default/files/publications/p0a09.pdf

Schlechty, P. C. (2011). *Engaging students: The next level of working on the work.* San Francisco, CA: Jossey-Bass.

Shute, R. W., & Webb, C. D. (1989). *Docsemur Docendo: In teaching we are taught.* The Journal of Professional Studies (Winter), 27–31.

Shute, W. R. (1989). Implications of preparing school administrators: Mentoring. American Educational Research Association. March 1989. San Francisco, CA.

Shute, J. W. (2009). *Expanding the truancy debate: Truancy, ethnic minorities and English language learners.* In M. Connolly & D. O'Keeffe (Eds.), *Don't fence me in: Essays on the rational truant* (pp. 115–138). Buckingham, UK: The University of Buckingham.

Shute, J. W., & Cooper, B. S. (2014). *Fixing truancy now: Inviting students back to class.* New York: Rowman & Littlefield.

Shute, J. & Cooper, B. S. (2014). Understanding in-school truancy: It may not be the student-but the curriculum, teacher, and pedagogy that is perpetuating truancy. Phil Delta Kappan.

Shute, R. W., & Webb, C. D. (1989). Docemur Docendo: In teaching we are taught. *The Journal of Professional Studies* (Winter), 27–31.

Skinner, J. (2009). *The Koblenz Model within Anglo-American Cultural Studies at German Universities.* Retrieved from http://www.developingteachers.com/articles_tchtraining/koblenzpf_jody.htm

Smith, T. (1997). Transforming a non-reading culture. In G. Jacobs, C. Davis, & W. Renandya (Eds.), Successful strategies for extensive reading (pp. 30–43). Singapore: SEAMEO Regional Language Centre.

Smith, F. (1988). *Joining the literacy club: Further essays into education.* Portsmouth, NH: Heinemann.

Sousa, D. A. (2011). *How the brain learns.* (4th ed). Thousand Oaks, CA: Corwin Press.

Teaiwa, T. (2011). Preparation for deep learning. *The Journal of Pacific History, 46*(2), 214–220.

Trelease, J. (1982). *Read aloud handbook.* New York: Penguin.

Values.com. (n.d.). François Duc De La Rochefoucauld. Retrieved from http://www.values.com/inspirational-quotes/3339-nothing-is-more-contagious-than-example-and-no

Weimer, M. (2013). *Learner-centered teaching: Five key changes to practice.* San Francisco, CA: Jossey-Bass.

Yazzie-Mintz, E. (2010). *Charting the path from engagement to achievement: A report on the 2009 high school survey of student engagement.* Bloomington, IN: Indiana University Press.

Yero, J. L. (2010). *Teaching in mind: How teacher thinking shapes education* (2nd ed.). MindFlight Publishing.

Zull, J. (2002). *The art of changing the brain: Enriching the practice of teaching by exploring the biology of learning.* Sterling, VA: Stylus Publishing, LLC.

Chapter 9

The Future with Visionary Leadership in Education—Now!

Carlos R. McCray & Bruce S. Cooper

Effective leaders revisit and readjust their educational and instructional visions often, so that their institutions remain up-to-date, effective, and relevant. Such re-visioning requires constant reflectivity, which is a quality of mindfulness. Mindfulness and emotional intelligence frameworks are posited as a basis for this chapter's discussion. Emotional intelligence is the cornerstone of relationship building, which is paramount to healthy and productive interactions between leaders and their constituents—for example, teachers and their students.

"Reflective practice" is likewise important to develop a vision. And to revisit and readjust this vision, a leader must be involved, aware, and responsive. For emotional intelligence and mindfulness are both key bases for this chapter's discussion. In this book, we have suggested that visionary leaders help others find their passions. To help others to do so, leaders must be reflective and tap into their own passions. Relationship building is also discussed to build healthy relationships; thus, leaders must be emotionally intelligent and have the ability to read and respond to their constituents appropriately.

This concluding chapter "pulls the whole, full book together" and provides practical, useful advice and suggestions both to professors of education leadership and the students and candidates for leadership jobs themselves. The chapter will both tie the book together and get practical with useful advice. Conclusions point to the practical, successful future of the field of school leadership and improvement: Now is now, and the book is ready to do the job.

We know that school supervision requires some real "super vision" to make things work, and schools improve. Creating and supporting *visionary leadership in schools* now and into the future are important concerns and steps for U.S. education—and this book explains the concepts and the steps to giving every leader the super vision to work with vision, now. We hope this book points the way.

As Maurice J. Elias (2013) explains, "Believe and envision: leaders must have a core belief that can be communicated with clarity, concision and passion. This is referred to as a bedrock *belief* and a compelling *vision*" (p. 3).

REFERENCES

Elias, M. J. (2013, July 18). 6 paths to better leadership. *Edutopia.* https://www.edu topia. org/blog/educators-improving-school-leadership-maurice-elias

Murphy, J. (2015). *Connecting teacher leadership to school improvements*. Thousand Oaks, CA: Corwin Press.

Index

African American Students in Urban Schools: Critical Issues and Solutions for Achievement (Moore and Lewis), 71
Arends, R. I., 103

Baker, B. D., 27
Bandura, Albert, 89, 98
Basham, J. D., 39
Beachum, F. D., 67, 69, 71, 74–75
Bell, Andrew, 101
Besser, L., 16
brain: faulty metaphor of, 106–7; mindfulness practices benefit to, 57–58; student engagement connections in, 108–9
Broderick, P., 56
budget (school district), 23; as educational plan, 21; local property tax burdens of, 21–22; revenue sources for, 21; TELs limitations on, 26
Burrows, L., 61
Bush, T., 51

Campsen, L., 17
Cantrell, T., 56
CARE. *See* Cultivating Awareness and Resilience in Education

Carter, R. A., 40, 41
CEC. *See* Council for Exceptional Children
Center for Public Education (CPE), 66
Center on Online Learning and Students with Disabilities (COLSD), 39
The Century Foundation report, 66
COLSD. *See* Center on Online Learning and Students with Disabilities
Comenius, John, 100
Common Core Standards, 7, 79
Connors, R., 9
Council for Exceptional Children (CEC): congressional recommendations of, 33; parental revoking consent opposition of, 33–34
Cox, T., Jr., 65
CPE. *See* Center for Public Education
Cultivating Awareness and Resilience in Education (CARE), 61–62
culturally relevant leadership, 71
Curios, George, 2
Current Issues in Education, 70
curriculum: big four core courses in, 79; character development of students in, 88–89; collaboration as innovation in, *80*, 81, 85; collaboration goals in, 85, *86*; diffusion process in, 85;

115

fears and hurdles in, *82*; hidden, 83, *84*; historical decisions about, 79–80; innovation definition in, 83; integration in, *86*, 86–87; integration trajectory of teaching in, *93*; key components of, 81, 83; learned, 83, *84*; learner-centered collaboration and integration model for, *88*; learning as focus in, 94; null, 83, *84*; open innovations concept in, 90; overcoming fears in, 81; as process and journey, *80*, 81; real-world problem solving in, 87–88; recommended, 83, *84*; reforms in, 79–80; self-efficacy building of students in, 89; stakeholder resistance in, 83; student-centered classroom in, 85–86; student voice in, 89; supported, 83, *84*; taught, 83, *84*; teacher access to experts in, 90–91; teacher and stakeholder collaboration in, 89–90; teacher model for collaboration and integration in, *92*; teacher proficiency levels in, 93–94; teacher use of integration in, *91*, 91–92; technology pull impacting, 85; tested, 83, *84*; written, 83, *84*

Department of Education, U.S., 33–34
Dewey, J., 52
Didactica Magna (Comenius), 100
diversity: *The Century Foundation* report on, 66; Cox on, 65; cultural collision and collusion in, 70; culturally relevant leadership for, 71; demographic change impacting, 66–67; empowerment in, 74; general welfare promotion in, 68; Gordon on, 65; introspection in, 73–74; "juvenocracies" in, 70; leadership elements in, *72*; leadership vision for, *73*; liberty and justice language in, 68; McCray and Beachum on, 74–75; Preamble to the Constitution of the United States and Pledge of Allegiance regarding, 67–68; -related scholarship in, *69*; respect in, 68; schools role in, 66; self-development pedagogy in, 70–71; self-realization in, 71; social justice leadership in, 72; students of color percentages in, 67; twentieth century problem in, 65; vision of, 66, 68–69
Downes, T. A., 25–26
DuBois, W. E. B., 65
DuFour, R., 5, 8–13
Duncan, Arne, 1

education, 21, 27, 32; common core standards mastery in, 7; corporal punishment use in, 35; Duncan on, 1; high school graduates regarding, 7–8; implementation gap in, 8; increased need of, 7; racial and socioeconomic gaps in, 7. *See also* online education
Einstein, Albert, 110
Elementary and Secondary Education Act (ESEA), 32
Elias, Maurice J., 114
ESEA. *See* Elementary and Secondary Education Act
ESSA. *See* Every Student Succeeds Act
Evans, H., 9
Every Student Succeeds Act (ESSA), 31, 43; as federal education law, 32; key provisions of, 32–33; mission of, 5

FAPE. *See* free appropriate public education
Farmer, Paul, 2
Figlio, D. N., 25–26
Fischel, W., 27–28
Frank, J. L., 56
free appropriate public education (FAPE), 33, 39
Froebel, Frederick, 83
Fullan, M. F., 9

Gabriel, John, 2
Generation X: work approach of, ix; worldview of, viii

Generation Y (Millennials): as first "digital natives," viii; as teachers, viii–ix; work approach of, ix
Generation Z (Zeds): characteristics of, ix; as internet and social media natives, ix
George, Bill, 56–57
Gordon, E. W., 65
Government Product Accessibility Template, 42
Green, P., 27

Haberman, M., 105
Haller, E. J., 68
Hargreaves, A., 80
Harris, A., 51
Hedberg, P. R., 52, 60
Herrington, D., 57
Hickman, C., 9
Hopkins, D, 51
Hoy's M-scale inventory, 57

IDEA. *See* Individuals with Disabilities Education Act
IDTs. *See* instructional data teams
IEP. *See* Individualized Education Program
iNACOL V2. *See* National Standards for Quality Online Teaching Version 2
Individualized Education Program (IEP), 32–34, 39
Individuals with Disabilities Education Act (IDEA), 32; benchmarks and short-term objectives elimination of, 34; CEC recommendations for, 33; federal funds allocation under, 34; inclusion practices in, 31; non-attorneys in due process hearings of, 33–34; parental consent revoking in, 33; physical restraint and seclusion in, 34–35; school leaders guideline recognition of, 39
instructional data teams (IDTs), 6; common assessment use in, 14; configurations of, 15–16; continuous improvement cycle steps for, 15; feedback in, 16; four C's monitoring of, 17; instruction impact focus in, 15; roles in, 16; school leader role in, 16–17; teacher collaboration in, 14; teacher resistance in, 16
internal accountability, 5, 7, 9, 12, 51
International Association of K-12 Online Learning, 41

Jung, Carl, 99
"juvenocracies," 70

Kabat-Zinn, Jon, 54, 55
Kearney, W. S., 57
Kelsey, C., 57
Kohls, N., 57
Kottkamp, R. B., 52, 53
Kouzes, J., 9

La Rochefoucauld, François Duc De, 99
Leana, C. R., 9
Learning to Teach (Arends), 103
LEAs. *See* local educational agencies
Leithwood, K., 6, 51
Lemov, Doug, 104
Lewis, C. W., 71
local educational agencies (LEAs), 33–35
Louis, K. S., 6
Lucas, T., 67

Martin, Jean-Pol, 102
Marzano, R., 5, 9, 13
Mattos, M., 5–6
MBSR. *See* Mindfulness-Based Stress Reduction
McCray, C. R., 67, 69, 71, 74–75
McLaughlin, M. W., 9–10
McNulty, B., 16
Meiklejohn, J., 61, 62
Metz, S., 56
Mindfulness-Based Stress Reduction (MBSR), 55, 56, 61

mindfulness practices, 113; brain benefits of, 57–58; CARE and SMART use in, 61–62; clarity and focus in, 57; communication benefit of, 56; as creative cognitive process, 54; formal manifestations of, 59; George on, 56–57; health benefits of, 57; Hedberg on importance of, 60; Hoy's M-scale inventory use in, 57; leadership preparation programs including, 60–62; making time for, 59–60; MBSR use in, 55, 56, 61; meaning of, 54; nonjudgmental aspect of, 58; origins of, 55; practices of, 56; reflective practices shared features with, 58–59, *59*; remaining present in, 56; rumination and, 58; school culture and student outcome improvement with, *61*; self-regulation of attention in, 54; social and emotional competence in, 61; student benefits of, *61*, 61–62; teacher benefits of, 56, *61*, 61–62; thought and experience acceptance in, 54–55
Miner, B., 8
Moore, J. L., III, 71
Most Likely to Succeed, 86
Murphy, E., 40
Murphy, J., 105

National Center for Education Statistics, 79
National Standards for Quality Online Teaching Version 2 (iNACOL V2), 41, *42*
NCLB. *See* No Child Left Behind Act
Nestojko, J. F., 101–2
New Jersey's 2.0% cap, 22–23, 27–28; flexibility lack in, 26; state educational aid cuts in, 25
No Child Left Behind Act (NCLB), 5, 32, 43

online education: accessibility in, 39–40; accommodation in, 39; collaboration in, 40–41; COLSD report on, 39; disabled students challenges in, 38–39; growth of, 38; IEP incorporation in, 39; iNACOL V2 use in, 41, *42*; parental involvement in, 41; school leaders research and resources for, 41–43; student interaction limitations in, 40; teacher contact limitations in, 40; teacher support lack in, 40; UDL use in, 42–43; VPAT use in, 41–42; WCAG in, 39–40
Ortiz, K., 39
Osterman, K. F., 52, 53
O'Sullivan, A., 23

Peery, A., 17
PLC. *See* professional learning community
Pledge of Allegiance, 67–68
Posner, B., 9
Postman, N., 105–6
Preamble to the Constitution of the United States, 67–68
"The Principal of Change: Stories of Learning and Leading" (Curios), 2
professional learning community (PLC), 8, 13, 17; clarity importance in, 11; collaborative culture of, 6, 10; data team structure in, 6; describing change in, 11–12; internal accountability in, 12; leadership team in, 12; purpose of, 10; results focus of, 10; role changes in, 11; school leader creation of, 6, 11–12; shared instructional leadership in, 8–9; six elements of, 10–11; student learning in, 10; team questions for, 10
Professional Standards for Educational Leaders, Standard I of, 3

Proposition 2.5, Massachusetts, 22, 24, 27; state aid in, 25; student enrollment in, 26
Proposition 13, California, 22, 24, 27; per pupil spending in, 25; Proposition 98's noncompliance with, 25

Read Aloud Handbook (Trelease), 99–100
Reeves, D., 8
reflective practices: actions and consequences consideration in, 52; as day-to-day experience, 53; decision mulling in, 53; Dewey on, 52; explicit knowledge and clear vision in, 53; Hedberg on importance of, 60; leadership preparation programs including, 60–62; making time for, 59–60; mindfulness shared features with, 58–59, *59*; Moscow exchange experience example of, 53; practice and professional growth connection in, 52; revisit and revise in, 52–53; school culture and student outcome improvement with, *61*; of school leaders, 52–53, 58–59, 113; student benefits of, 61–62; wise decision-making in, 52
Reibel, D., 56
Reynolds, M., 53
Rice, M. F., 39, 40, 41
Richards, C. E., 27
Rogers, E. M., 83, 85

Sauer, S., 57
school leaders, visionary: as boundary scanners, vii; characteristics of, vii; Curios steps and formula for, 2; different generations awareness of, vii–ix, vii–x; ESSA familiarity of, 33; IDEA guideline recognition of, 39; IDTs role of, 16–17; internal accountability culture creation of, 9; internal accountability questions for, 7; introduction of, 3; Leithwood and Louis on effective, 6; mindfulness practices of, 54–59, 113; multiple issues and constituents dealings of, 51; online education research and resources for, 41–43; open communication of, 2; PLC culture creation of, 6, 11–12; reflective practices of, 52–53, 58–59, 113; relationship building of, 57, 113; responsibilities and accountability increase of, 51; school reform accountability of, 5; shared or distributive leadership of, 9; student achievement impact of, 5–6, 51; "super vision" of, 1, 113–14; SWPBIS leadership practices for, 43–44; teachers capacity building of, 14; two philosophical practices of, 51–52; vision and mission statements developing of, 2; "visionary" concept in, 1; Zmorenski on, 1–2
school-wide positive behavioral interventions and supports (SWPBIS), 31–32; continuum building in, 35; core components of, 37; data use in, 37–38; expectations and outcomes in, 37; framework of, 35; implementation and sustainability in, 38; leadership practices for, 43–44; primary goal of, 35; Tier 2 supports in, 36; Tier 3 supports in, 37; universal behavior support in, 36
Schunk, D. H., 89
Schwartz, Jake, 44
self-development pedagogy, 70–71
Seneca, 100
Senge, Peter, 81
Sexton, T. A., 23
Sheffrin, S. M., 23
Shute, J. W., 102
SISP. *See* Specialized Instructional Support Personnel

SMART. *See* Stress Management and Relaxation Techniques
SMART goal (Strategic, Measurable, Achievable, Relevant, and Timely), 15
Smith, F., 98
Smith, S., 39
Smith T., 9
Soltis, J. F., 68
Specialized Instructional Support Personnel (SISP), 32
Stahl, S., 39
Stress Management and Relaxation Techniques (SMART), 61–62
Strike, K. A., 68
student engagement, vii, 110; active learning for, 108–9; brain connections in, 108–9; components of, 108; decline in, 97; "incidental" learning in, 98–99; knowledge mean making as, 100; learner identity in, 99; students teaching peers caveat in, 102–3; students teaching peers outcomes and benefits for, 102; students teaching peers principle and studies in, 101–2; "teacher example" and "teacher modeling" in, 98; teacher learning quest for, 99–100; teachers research-based skills mastery impacting, 103–4; teaching to learn practice for, 100–103; voyage of learning example for, 107–8
students, 67; -centered classroom curriculum, 85–86; character development of, 88–89; online education interaction limitations of, 40; PLC learning of, 10; reflective and mindfulness practices benefits of, *61*, 61–62; school leaders achievement impact on, 5–6, 51; self-efficacy building of, 89; TEL achievement impact on, 26–27; voice in curriculum of, 89

students, disabled: ESSA educational rights of, 32–33; inclusion challenges of, 31–32; online education challenges of, 38–39
Suzuki, D. T., 55
SWPBIS. *See* school-wide positive behavioral interventions and supports

Talbert, J. E., 9–10
tax expenditure limit (TEL), 22, 24–25; larger class size due to, 27; public education quality in, 27; student achievement impact of, 26–27; taxpayer expectations for, 26; taxpayer ownership reduced by, 27–28
teachers: belief systems of, 105; collaborative communities of, 9–10; data team structure for, 6; factory metaphor belief of, 106; faulty brain metaphor of, 106–7; IDTs collaboration and resistance of, 14, 16; leadership sharing of, 13; metaphor control of, 105; millennials as, viii–ix; mindfulness practices benefits of, 56, *61*, 61–62; Miner on turnover of, 8; online education and, 40; PLC results-oriented collaborative teams of, 12–13; Postman on classroom metaphors of, 105–6; research-based skills mastery of, 103–4; school leader capacity building of, 14; voyage of learning example in, 107–8. *See also* curriculum; student engagement
Teach Like a Champion: 62 Techniques that Put Students on the Path to College (Lemov), 104
TEL. *See* tax expenditure limit
traditional public school districts (TPSDs), 21, 26; budget votes in, 23; county property taxes in, 22–23; host municipality property taxes in,

22; programs and services offered by, 23–24; property tax reliance in, 23; TEL advocates claims toward, 24–25; TEL alternative actions of, 24; TEL restraints on, 28; TEL "triple whammy" on, 22

Trelease, Jim, 99–100

Universal Design for Learning (UDL), 42–43

Villegas, A. M., 67
Vince, R., 53
Voluntary Product Accessibility Template (VPAT), 41–42

Web Content Accessibility Guideline (WCAG) 2.0, 39–40
"Why Leaders Must Have Vision" (Zmorenski), 1
Williams, Joe, 44
Workforce Rehabilitation Act, Section 508, 39, 42

Yawn, C. R., 67
Yero, J. L., 105

Zeds. *See* Generation Z
Zen Buddhism, 55
Zmorenski, Debbie, 1–2

About the Editors

Bruce S. Cooper, PhD, is Professor Emeritus, Education Leadership, Administration and Public Policy, Graduate School of Education, Fordham University, New York. He also taught at the University of Pennsylvania and Dartmouth College, after receiving his doctorate at the University of Chicago, with Donald A. Erickson as his mentor. Cooper has written forty-four books on education politics and policy, including *The Handbook of Education Politics and Policy*, in two editions with Lance D. Fusarelli and James Cibulka. He served as president of the Politics of Education Association and a founding member of Private School Research Association. He received the Jay D. Scribner Award for Mentoring from the University Council for Education Administration.

Carlos R. McCray, EdD, is an associate professor at the University of Louisville in the Educational Leadership and Administration Program. He teaches qualitative research to aspiring educational leaders. Professor McCray is the coauthor of the books, *School Leadership in a Diverse Society: Helping Schools Prepare All Students for Success* and *Cultural Collision and Collusion: Reflections on Hip-Hop Culture, Values, and Schools*. He is also the co-editor of the books, *Mentoring with Meaning: How Educators Can be More Professional and Effective, Mentoring for School Quality*, and *Effective Education for All: Implementing Positive Behavior Support in Early Childhood through High School* with Bruce S. Cooper.

Stephen V. Coffin is a PhD candidate in education at the Graduate School of Education, Rutgers University; teaches school finance as an adjunct professor at the Graduate Schools of Education for Montclair State University and Rutgers University; teaches school and higher education finance and economics for the Fordham University Graduate School of Education; serves on three editorial review boards; publishes articles, reports, chapters, and books; is a former school business administrator; has earned an MBA in finance and MPA in public administration; and focuses his research on education finance and policy, charter schools, community economic development, school business administration, school choice, and equal educational opportunity and equity.

About the Contributors

Karen Andronico is an English teacher at Herbert H. Lehman High School located in Bronx, New York.

Selma K. Bartholomew Ph.D., is a researcher, published author, and a dynamic leader. She earned her doctorate degree in educational leadership, administration, and policy from Fordham University. She is a recognized as a Dr. Barbara Jackson Scholar by the University Council for Educational Administration. In addition, she holds a Master of Science in Education degrees from Adelphi University and Fordham University, and has pursued graduate studies in pure mathematics at The City University of New York (ABD).

Lisa Bass is assistant professor at North Carolina State University. Dr. Bass received her Ph.D. in Educational Leadership and Policy Studies and Comparative and International Education from the Pennsylvania State University. Her work focuses on education reform with an emphasis on equity and ethics, particularly the ethics of caring.

Floyd D. Beachum is the Bennett Professor of Urban School Leadership at Lehigh University. He is also the Program Director and an Associate Professor in the Educational Leadership program in the College of Education. He received his doctorate in Leadership Studies from Bowling Green State University. He also holds a Master's in Education and a Bachelor of Science in Social Studies Education from Alabama State University.

Kwang Sun C. Blair is associate professor in the Applied Behavior Analysis Program and the Positive Behavior Support Graduate Certificate Program of the Department of Child and Family Studies at the University of South

Florida and a Board Certified Behavior Analyst. Dr. Blair received her Ph.D. in special education and minor in psychology from the University of Arizona in 1996.

Su-Je Cho is associate professor of childhood special education in the Division of Curriculum and Teaching at the Fordham University Graduate School of Education. She coordinates the Childhood Special Education Program.

Ingrid Lafalaise is assistant principal at a New York City high school and has been an educator for over fifteen years. She has designed and taught curriculum in multiple content areas including math and science. Ingrid has also worked on the development and alignment of science standards at both a city and state level.

Holly Rittenhouse-Cea Ph.D., is adjunct professor and student teaching supervisor, Fordham University.

Jonathan W. Shute is assistant professor in the School of Education at Brigham Young University-Hawaii. He has over fifteen years teaching experience in elementary and secondary classrooms. He also has a strong background working with at-risk students, as well as English language learners and students from diverse ethnicities.

www.ingramcontent.com/pod-product-compliance
Lightning Source LLC
Chambersburg PA
CBHW030116010526
44116CB00005B/273